Real World
Colouring Book
For Advanced Users & Adults

50 Images

**Created From Real Life Photos
For You To Colour As You Please.**

ISBN 978-0-359-82292-8
90000
9 780359 822928

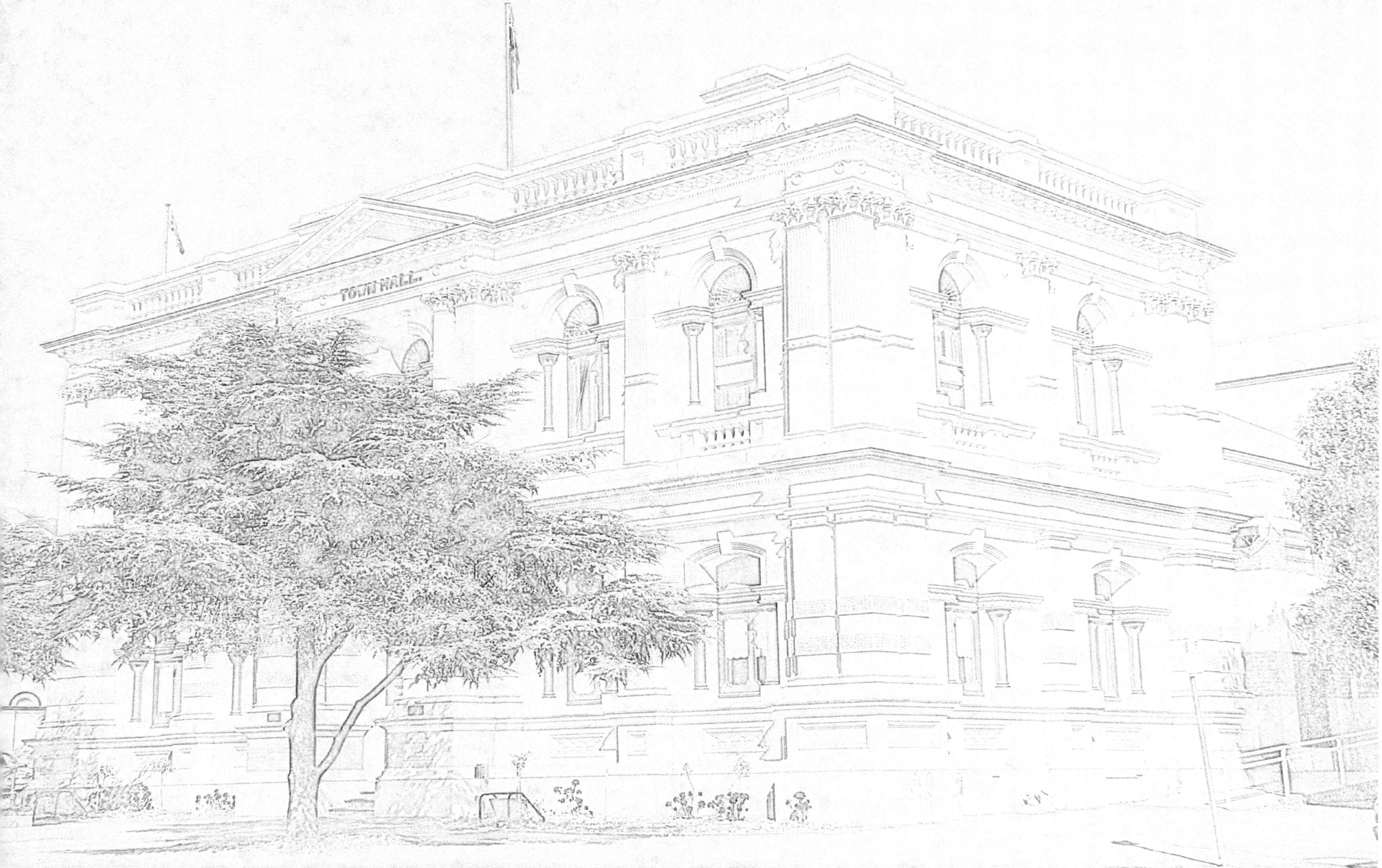
TOWN HALL.

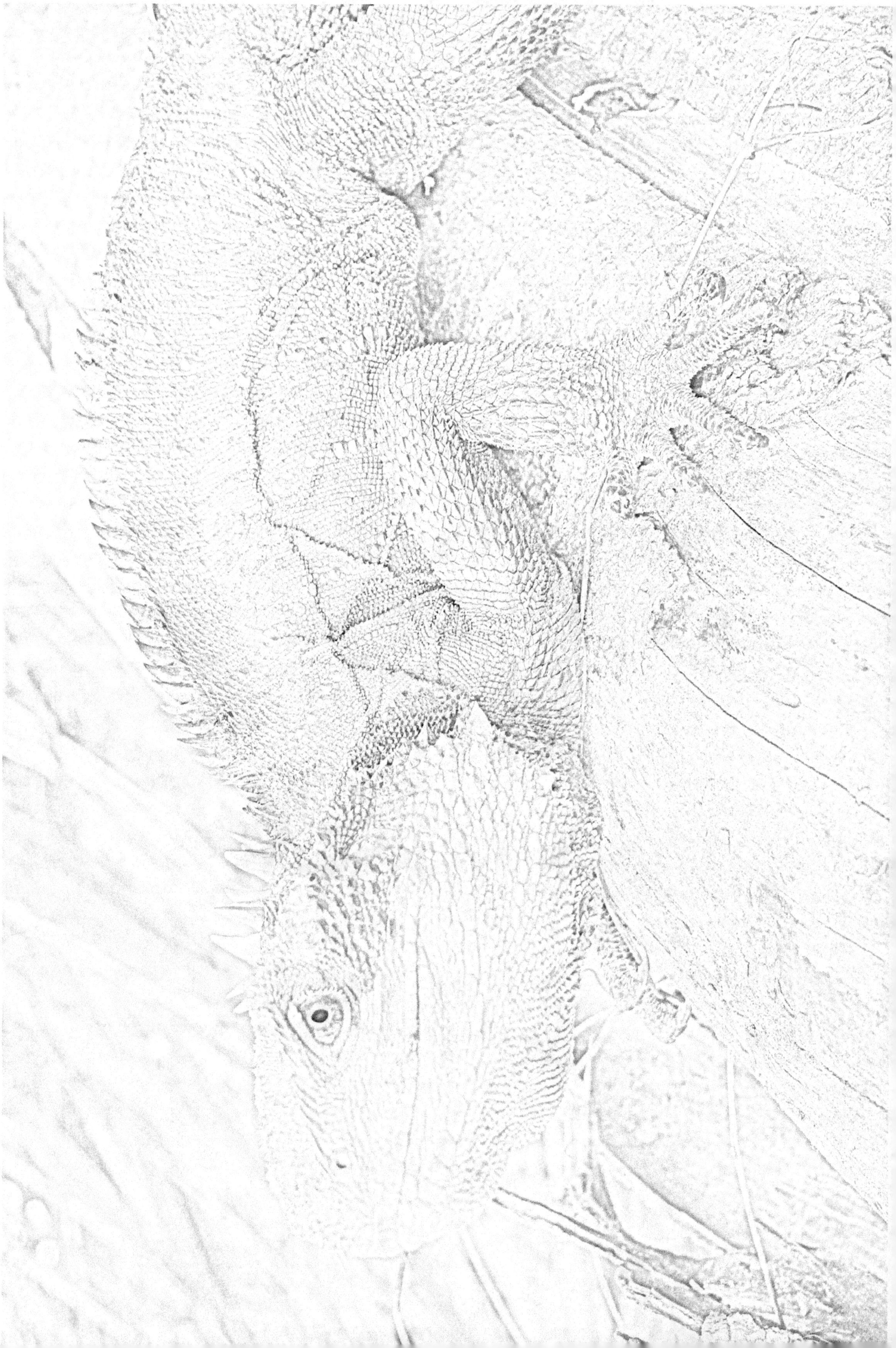

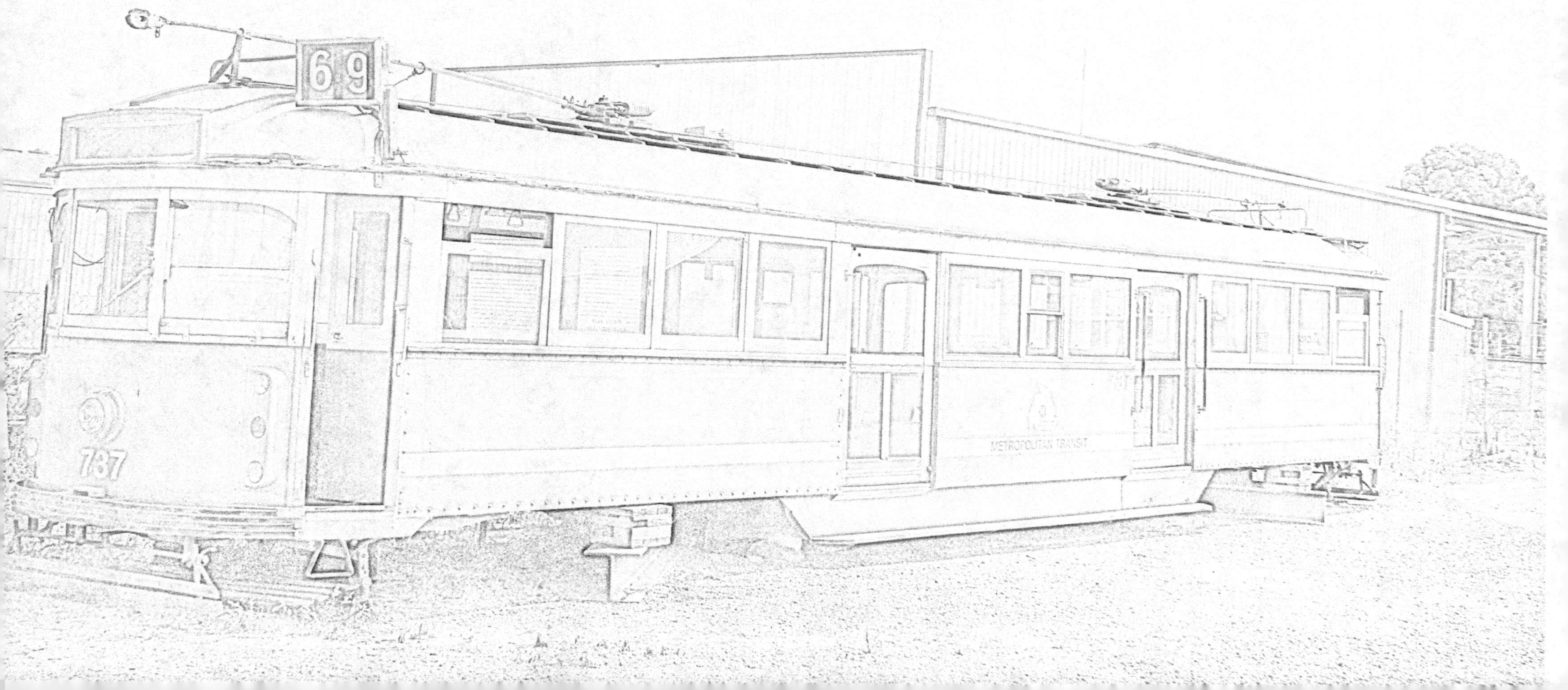
69
737
METROPOLITAN TRANSIT

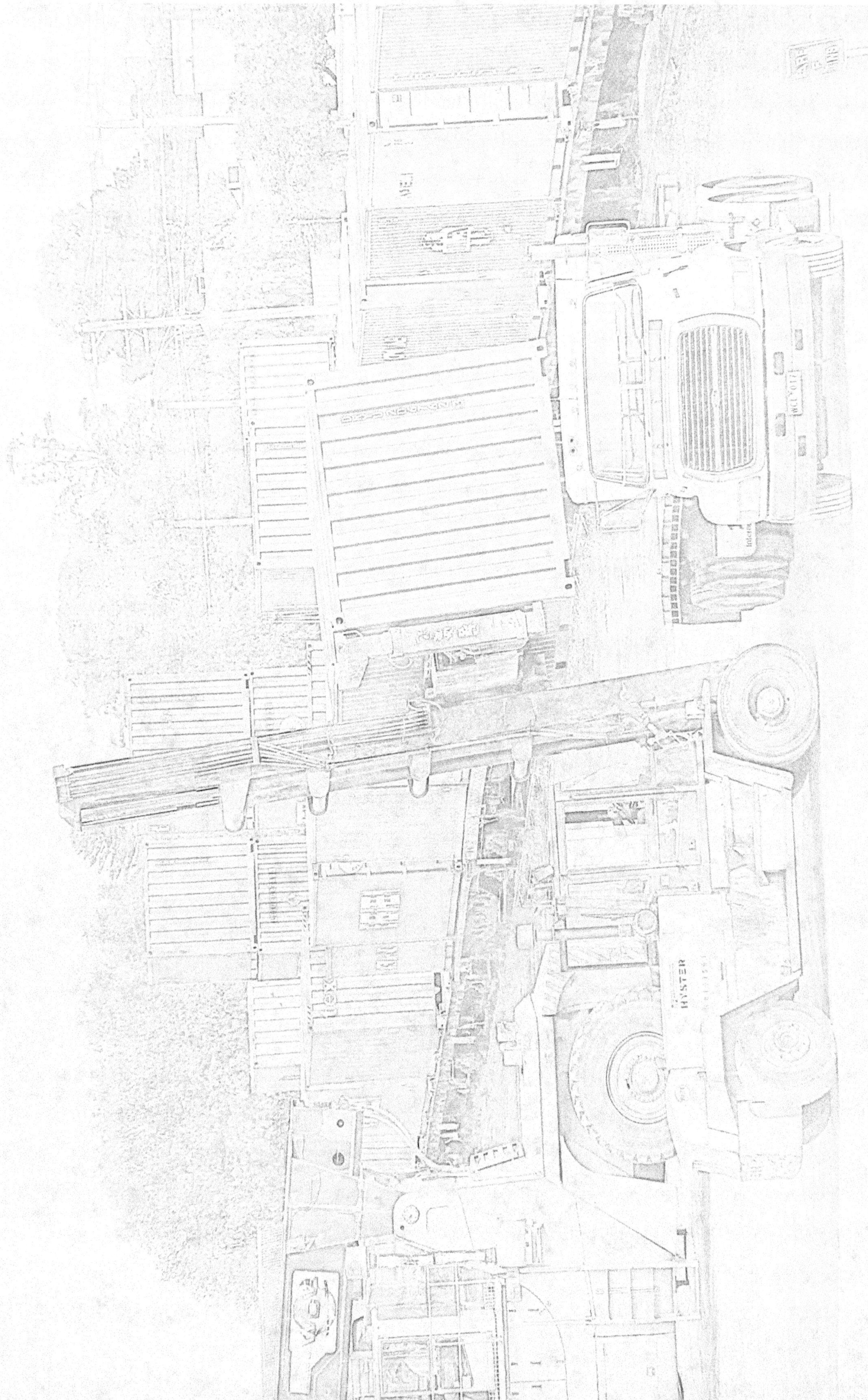
HYSTER

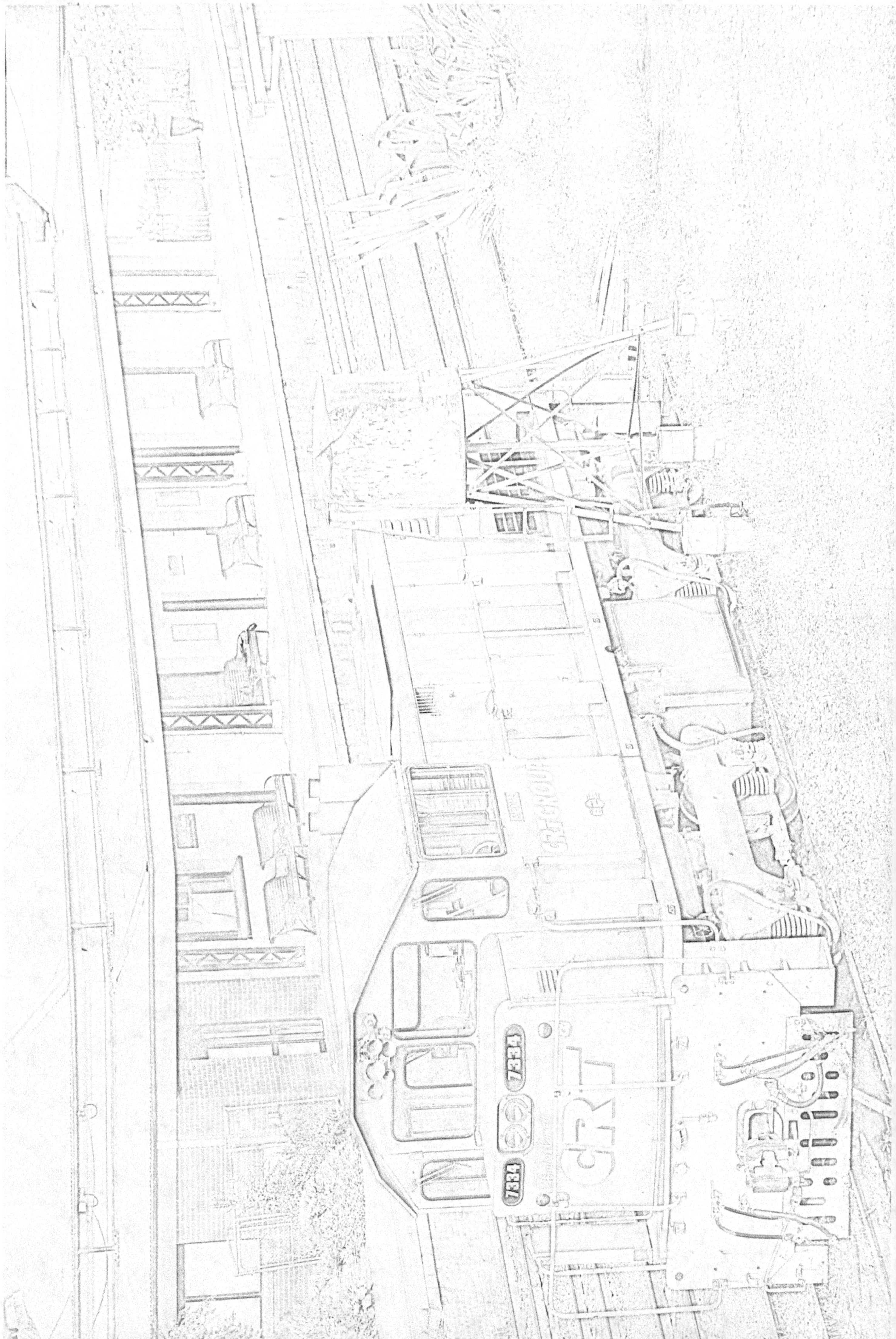
7334
7334

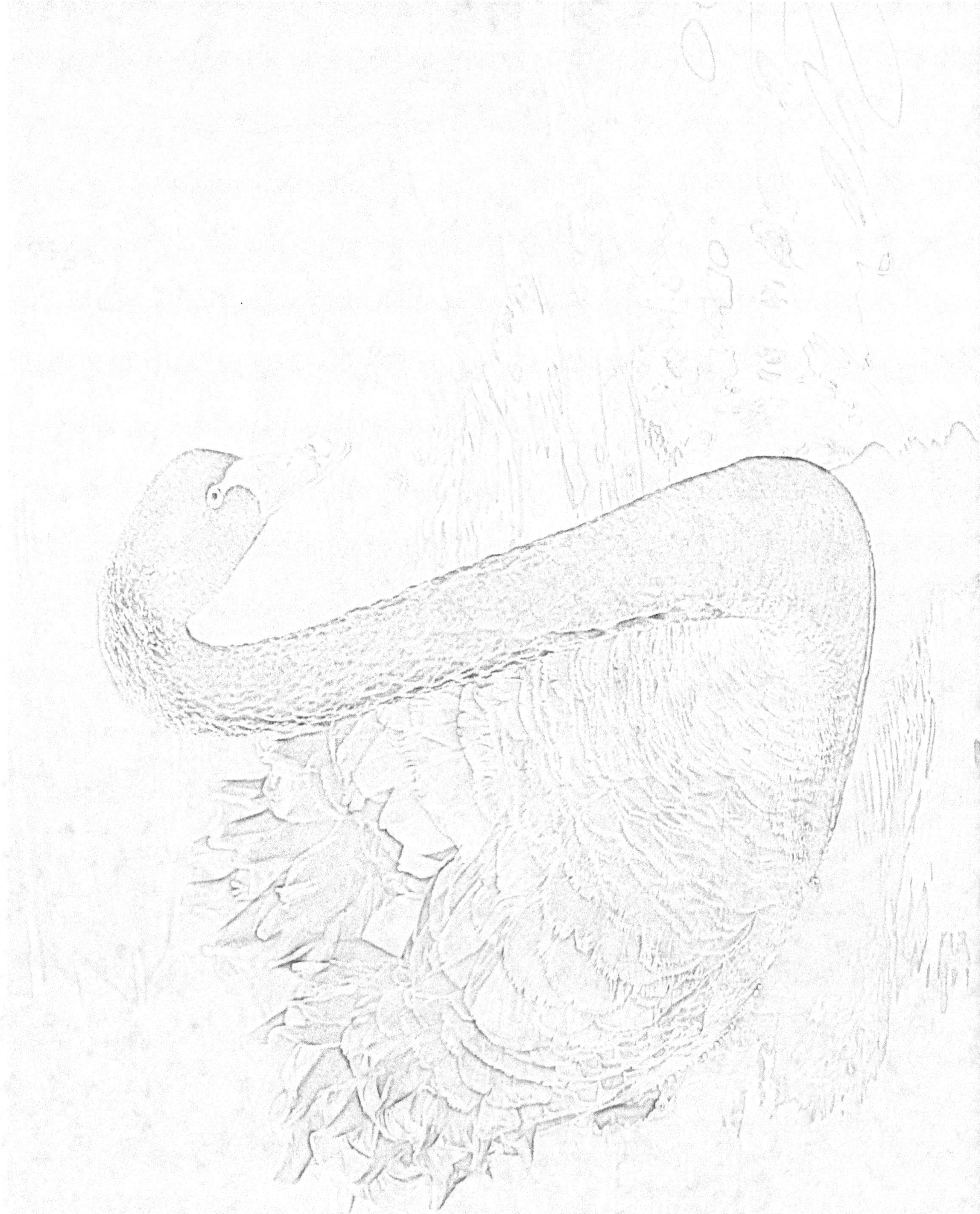

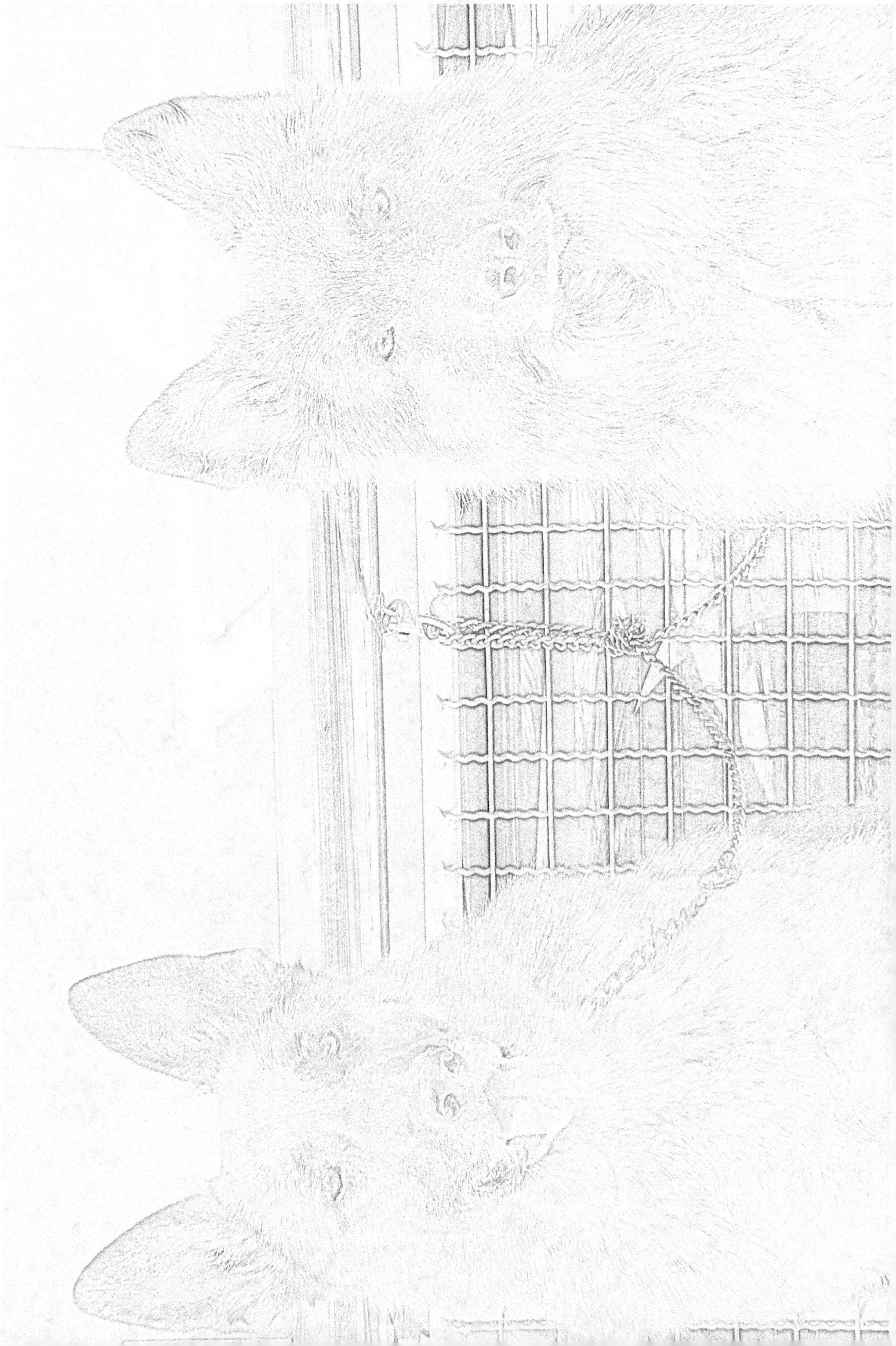

DRIVE
THRU
DRIVE
THRU
McDonald's
McDonald's
PTOMETRIST

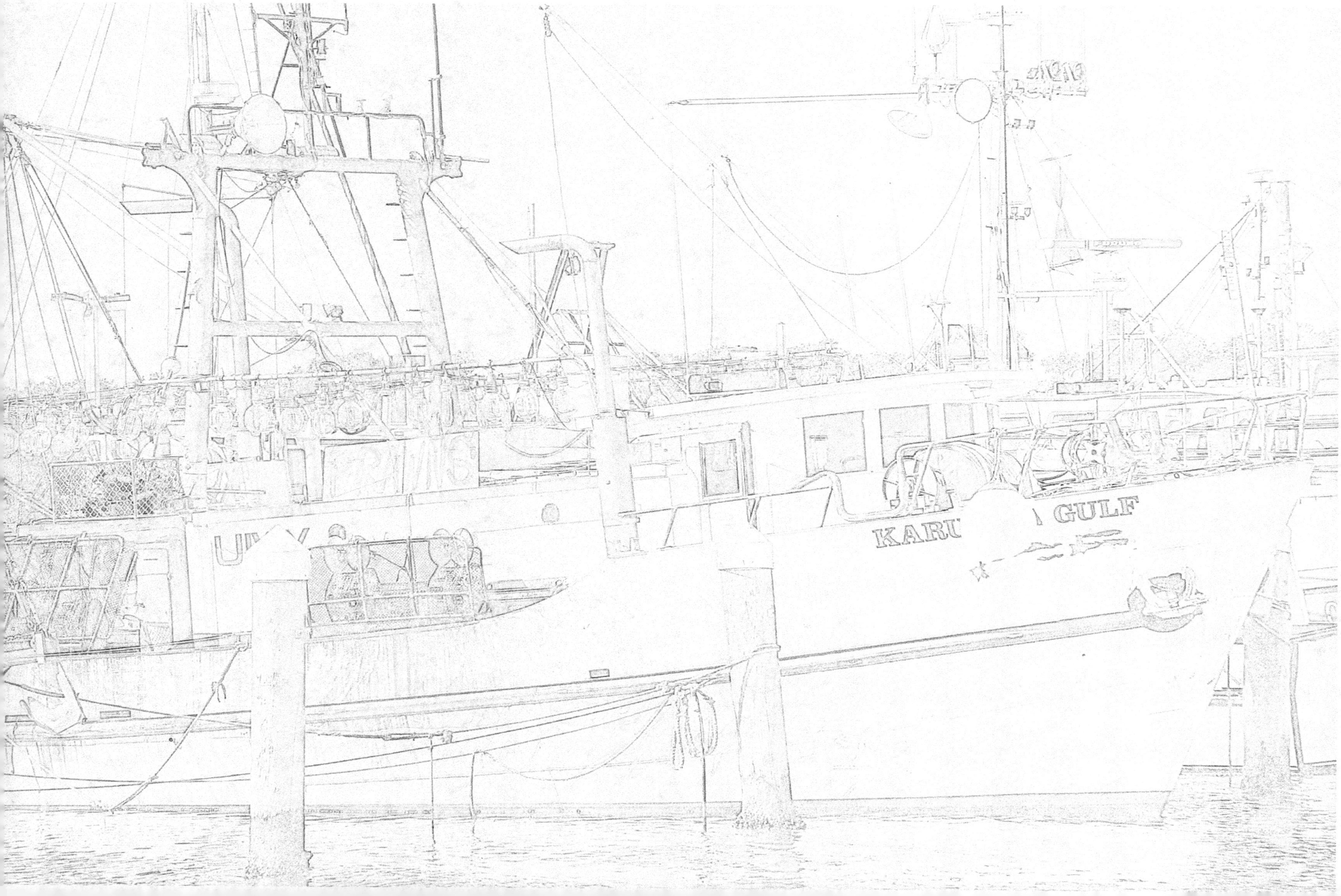

KARU
GULF

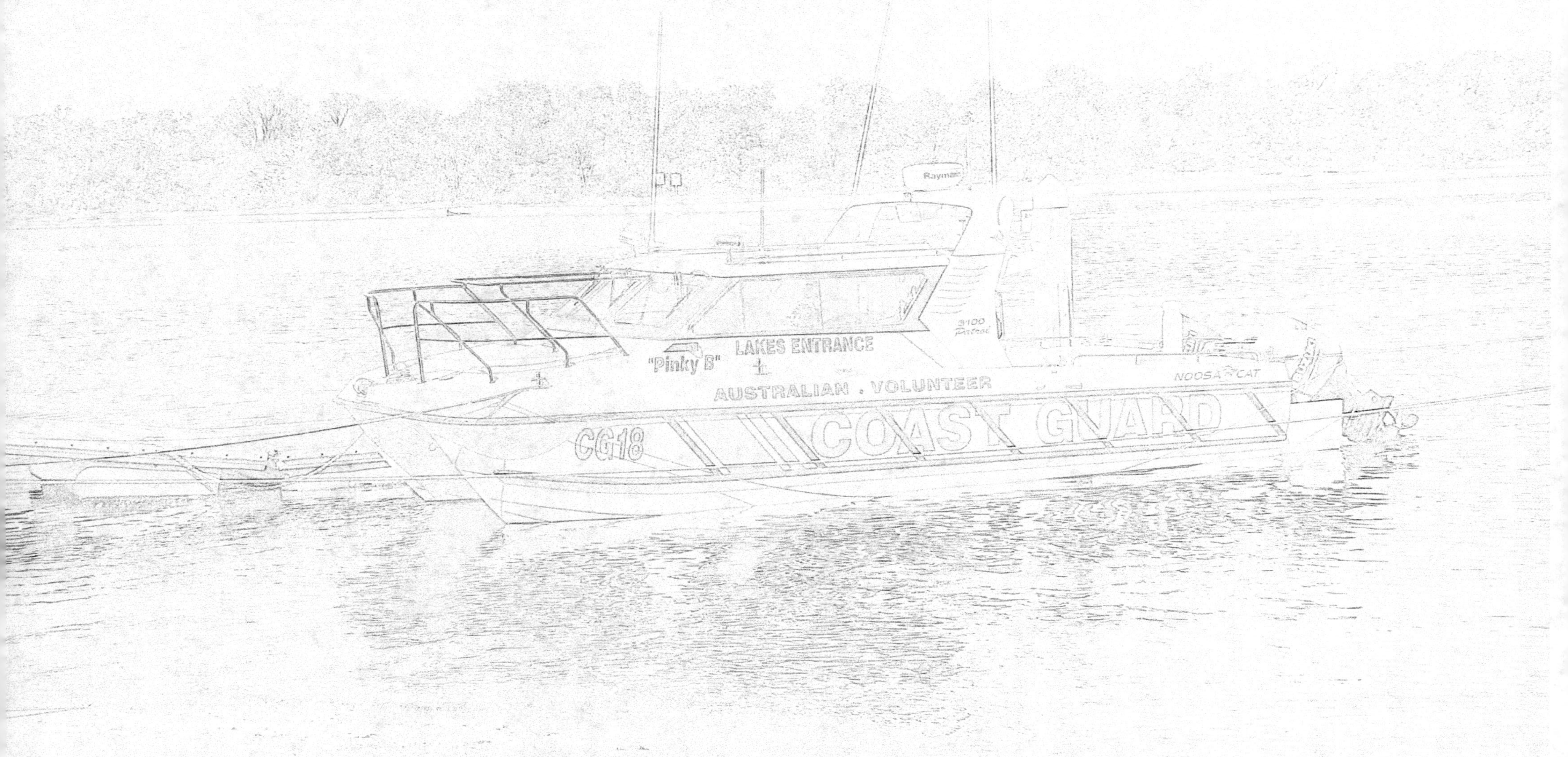
LAKES ENTRANCE
"Pinky B"
AUSTRALIAN . VOLUNTEER
CG18
COAST GUARD
3100
Patrol
NOOSA CAT

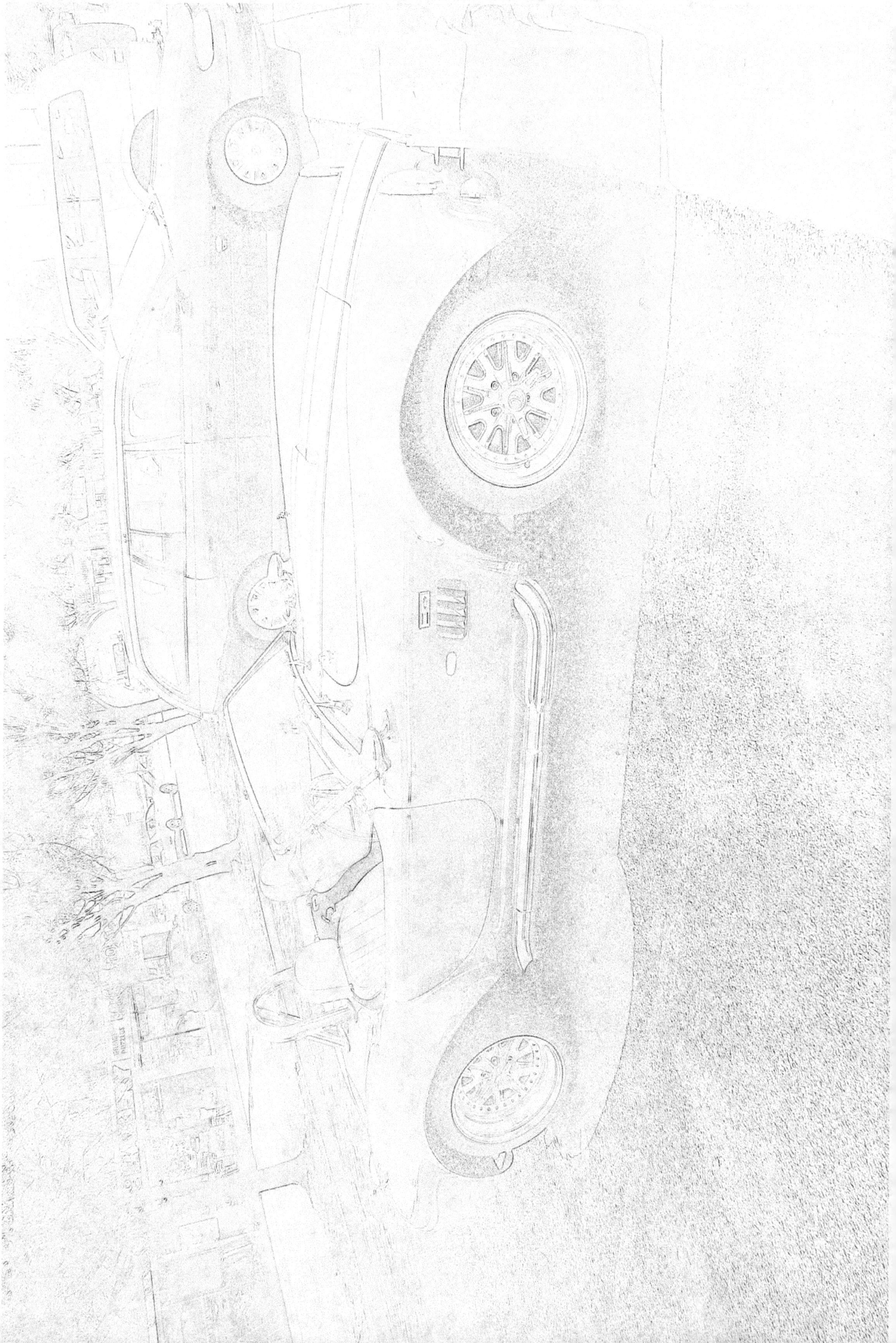

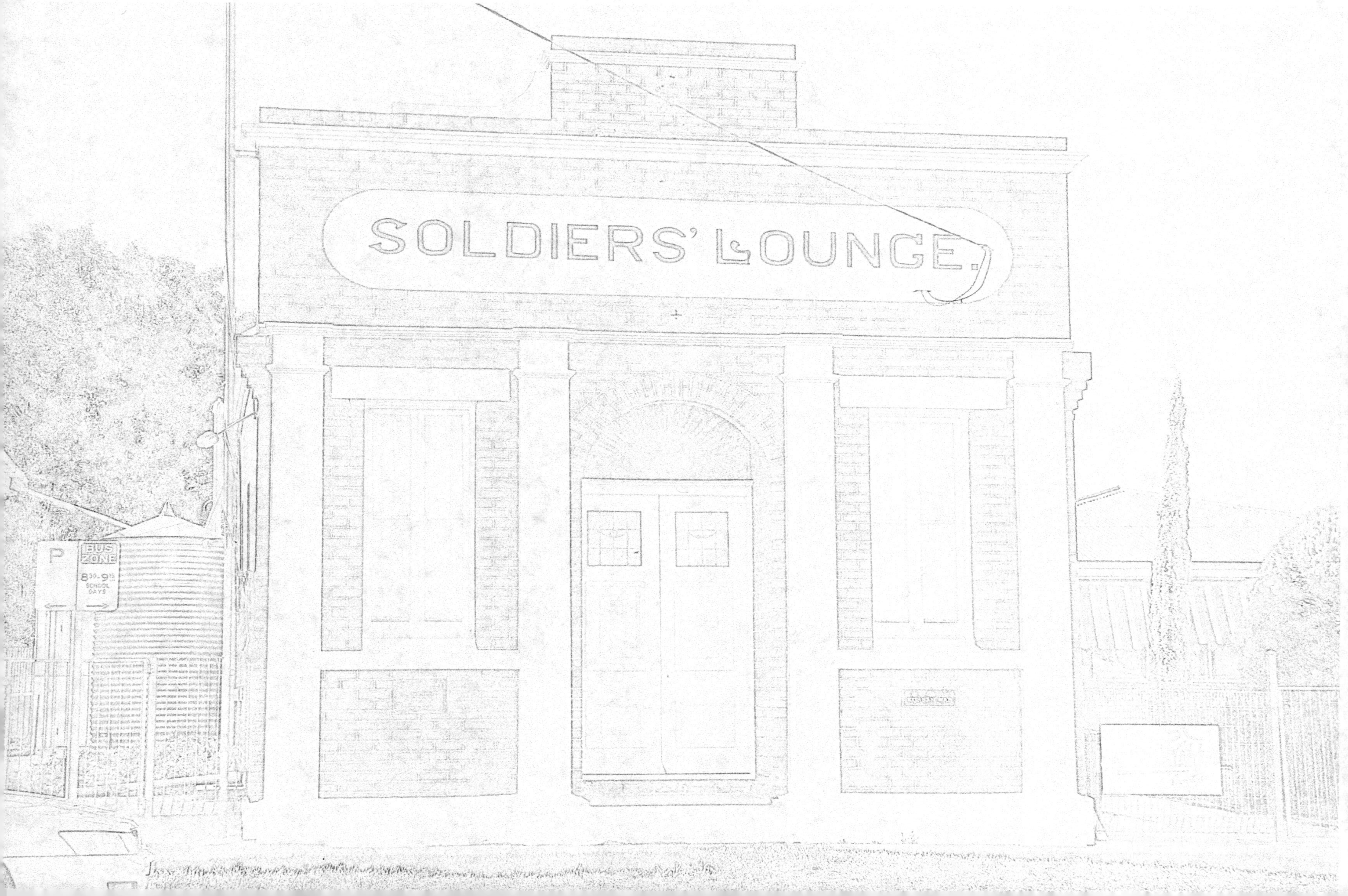
SOLDIERS' LOUNGE.
P
BUS ZONE
8³⁰-9¹⁵
SCHOOL DAYS

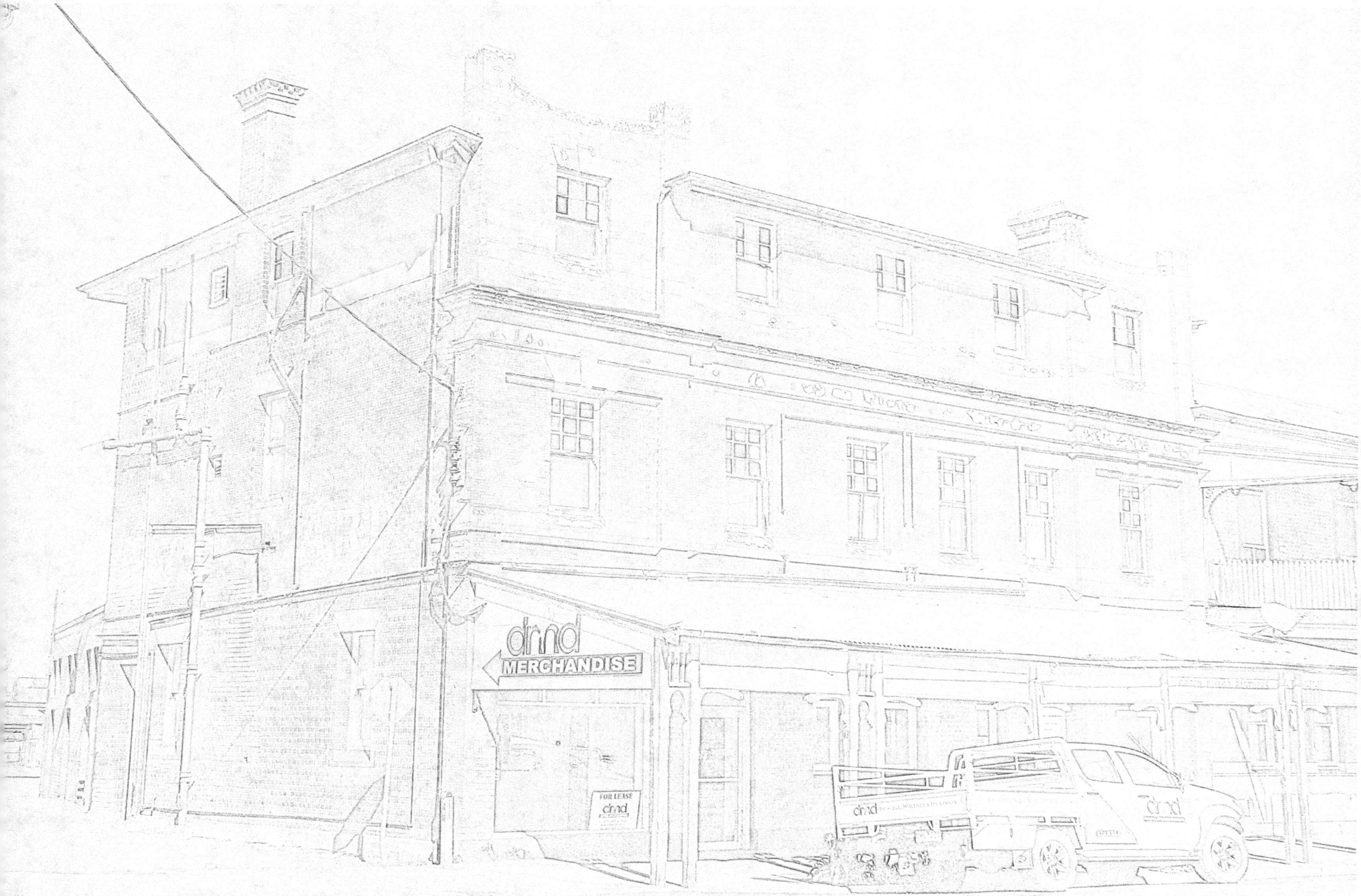
drnd
MERCHANDISE
FOR LEASE
drnd

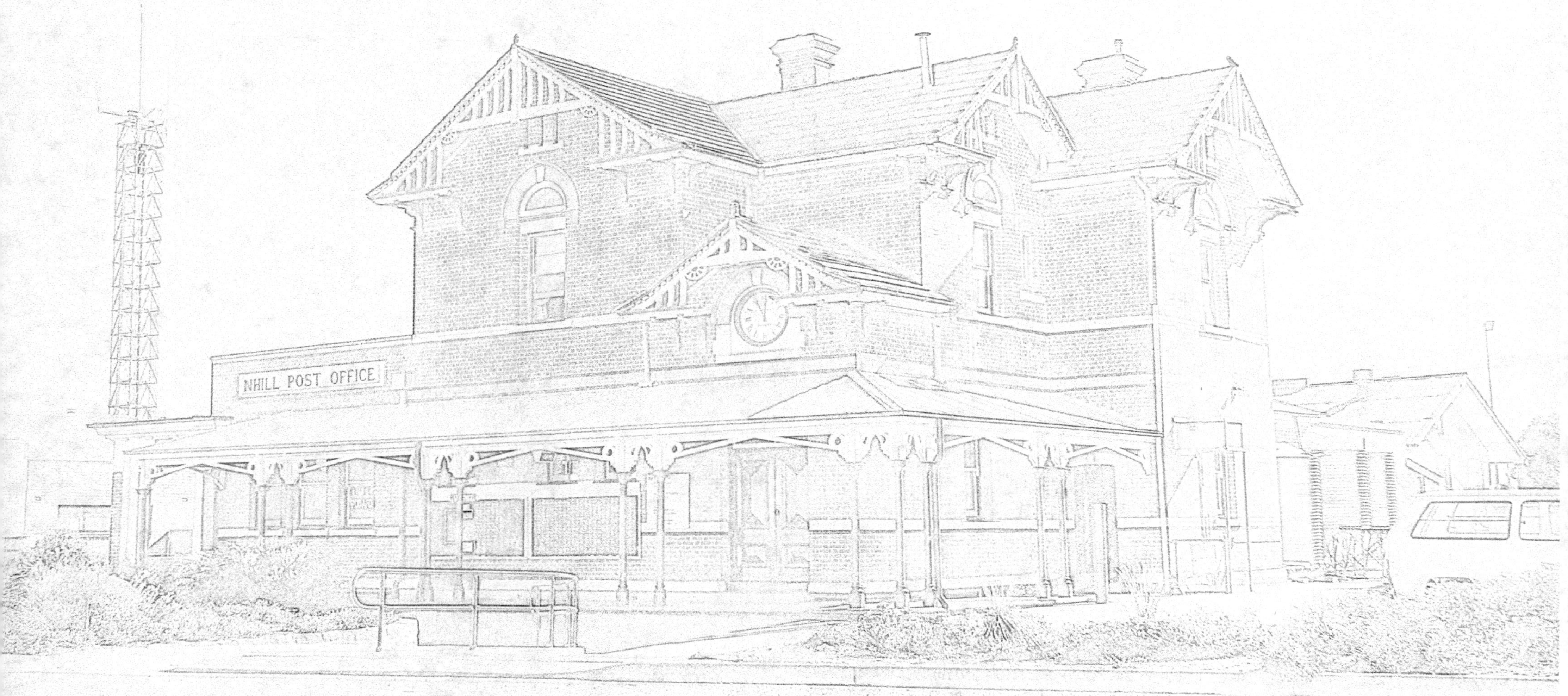
NHILL POST OFFICE

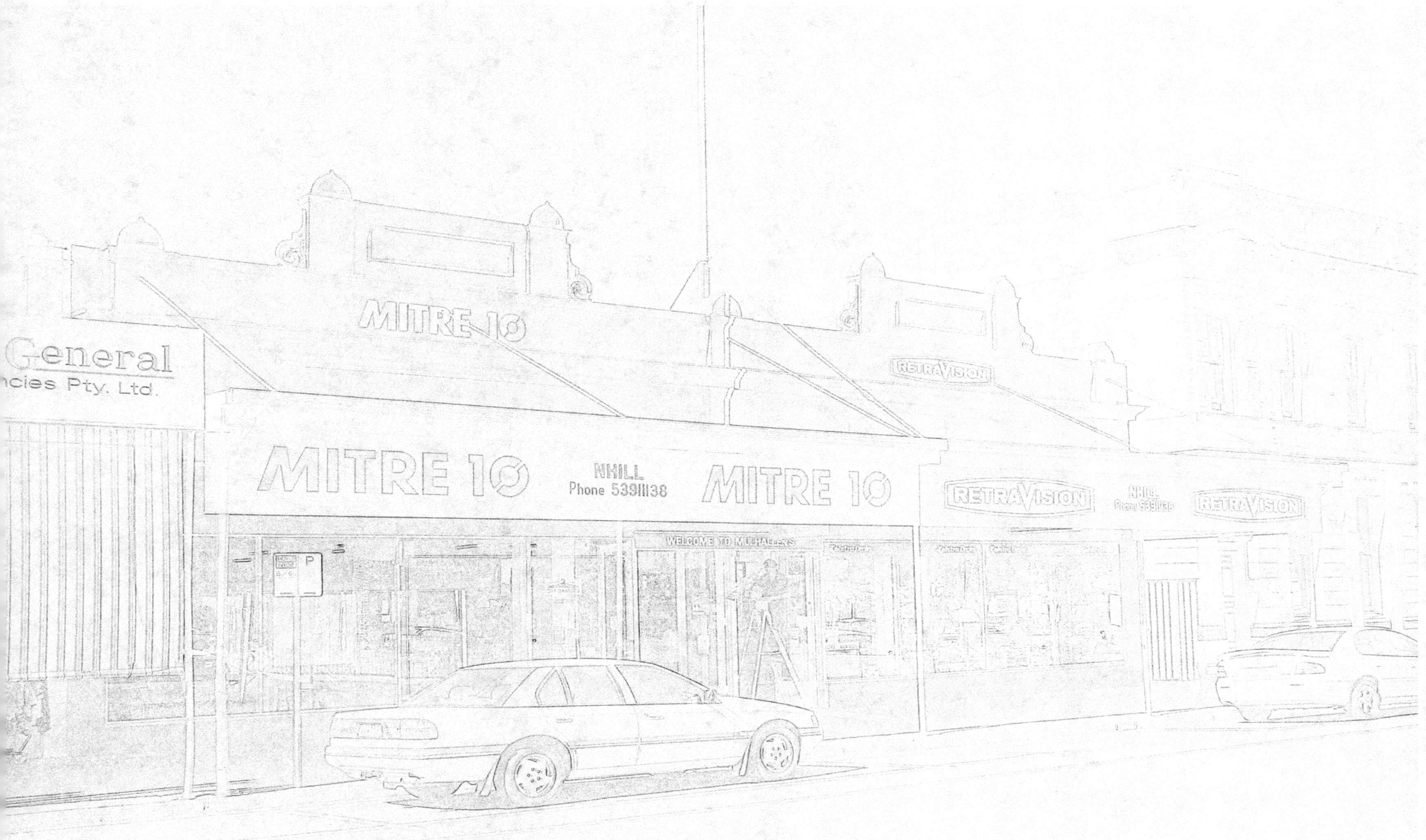
General
ncies Pty. Ltd.
MITRE 10
MITRE 10
NHILL
Phone 5391138
MITRE 10
WELCOME TO MULHALLEN'S
RETRAVISION
RETRAVISION
NHILL
RETRAVISION

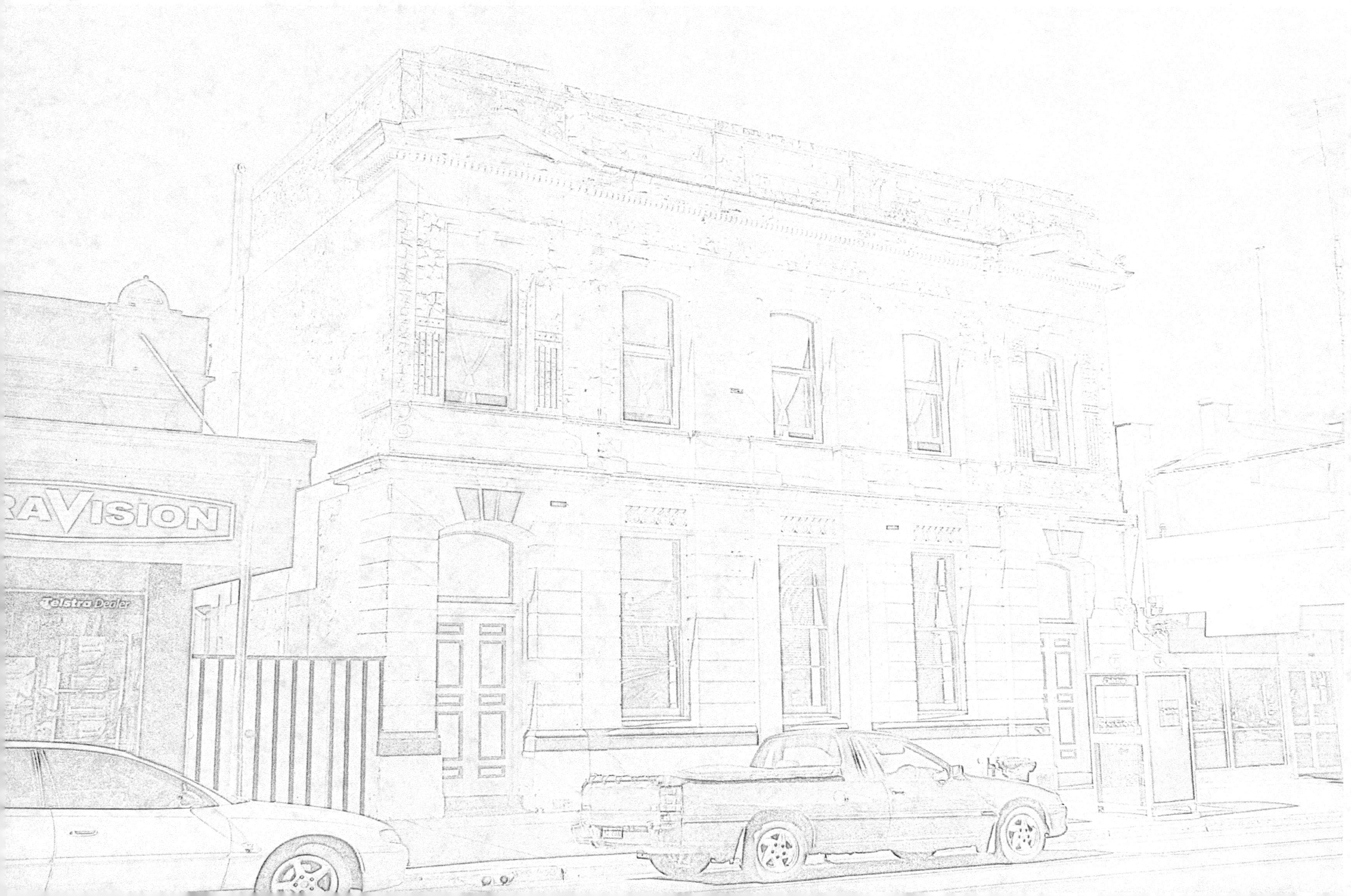
RAVISION
Telstra Dealer

RINTOULE'S
UNION
HOTEL
MILDARA
MEALS
7 DAYS
MAIN
BAR

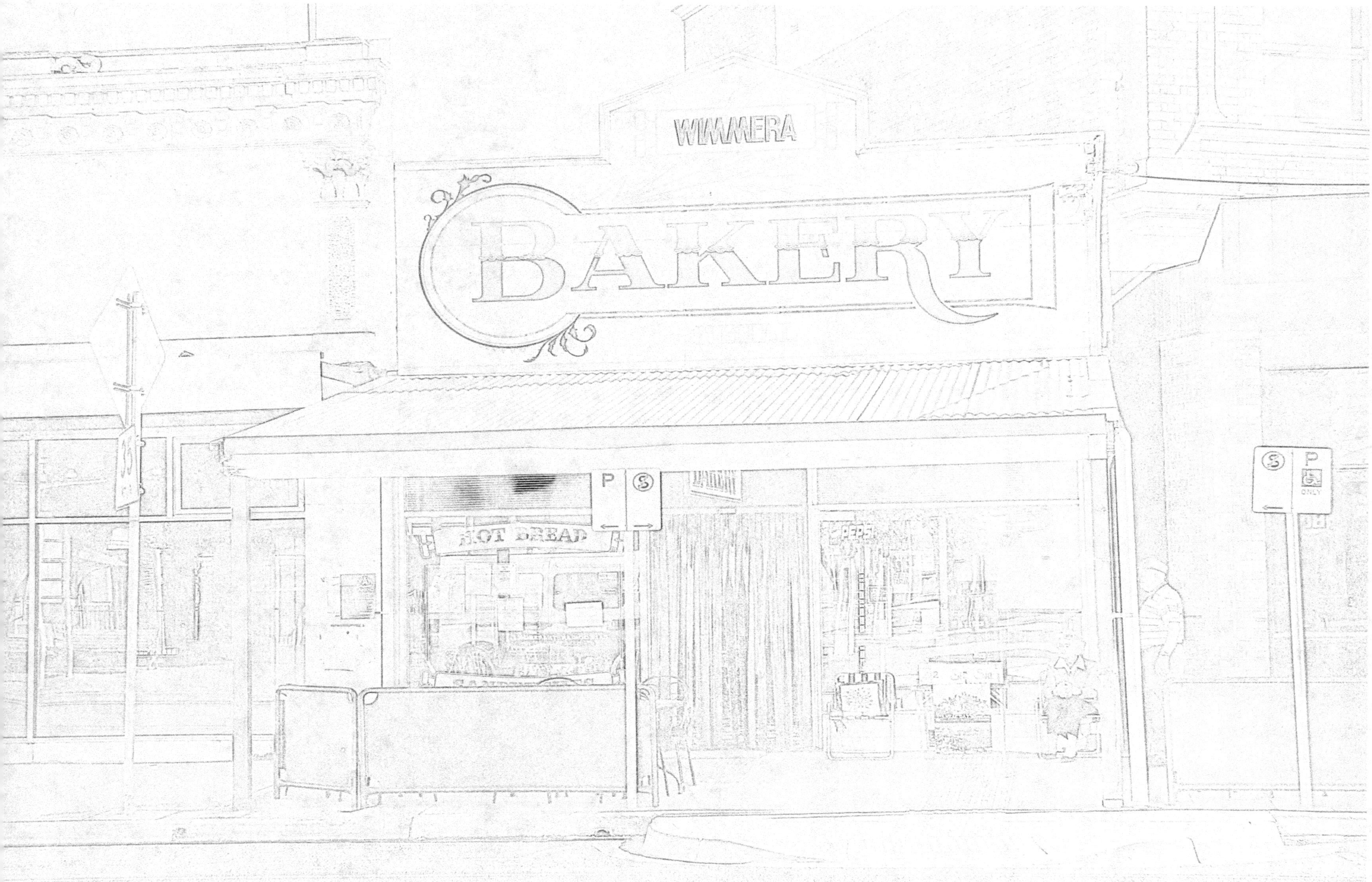
WIMMERA
BAKERY
HOT BREAD
ONLY

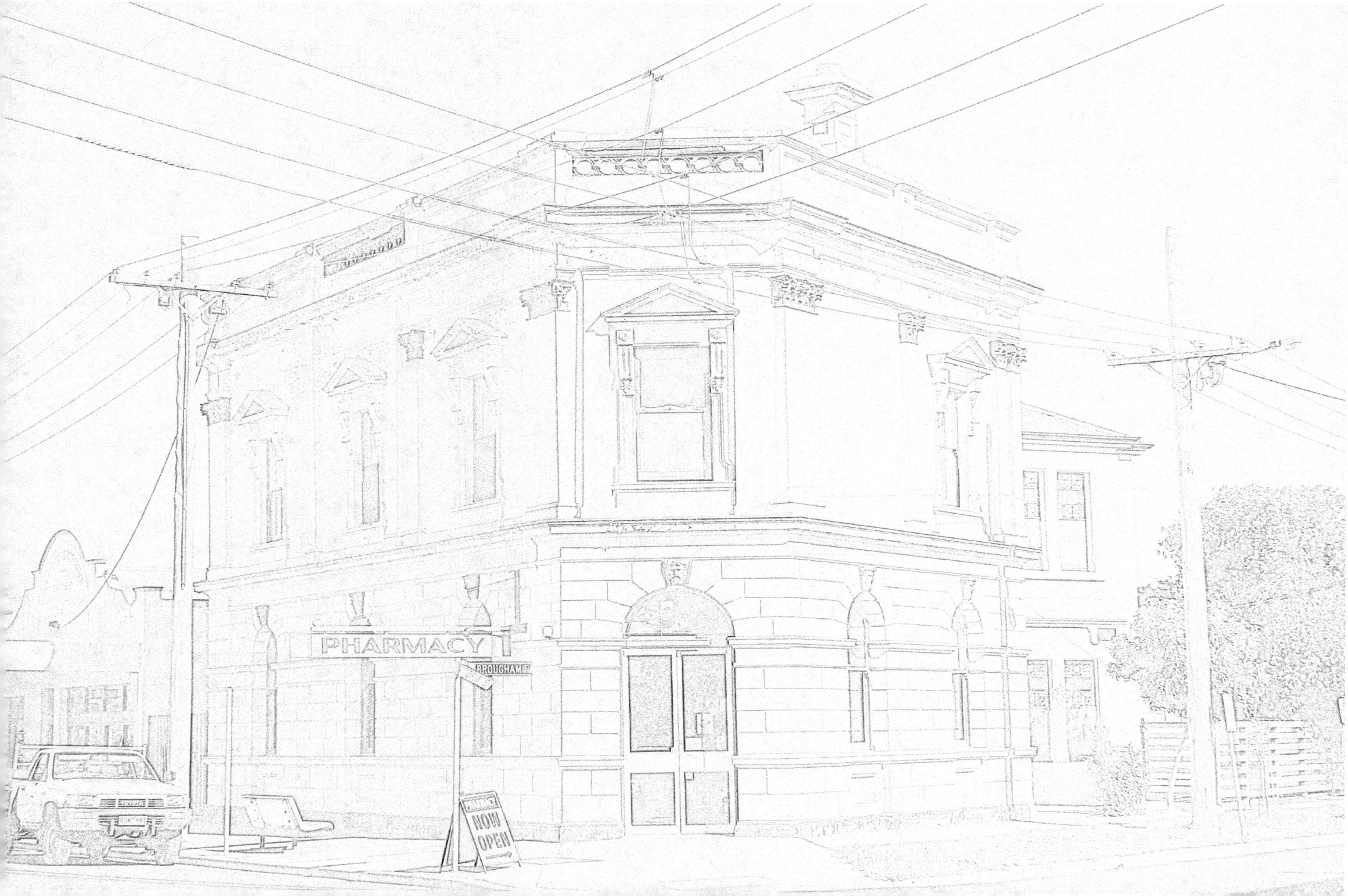
PHARMACY
BROUGHAM ST
NOW OPEN

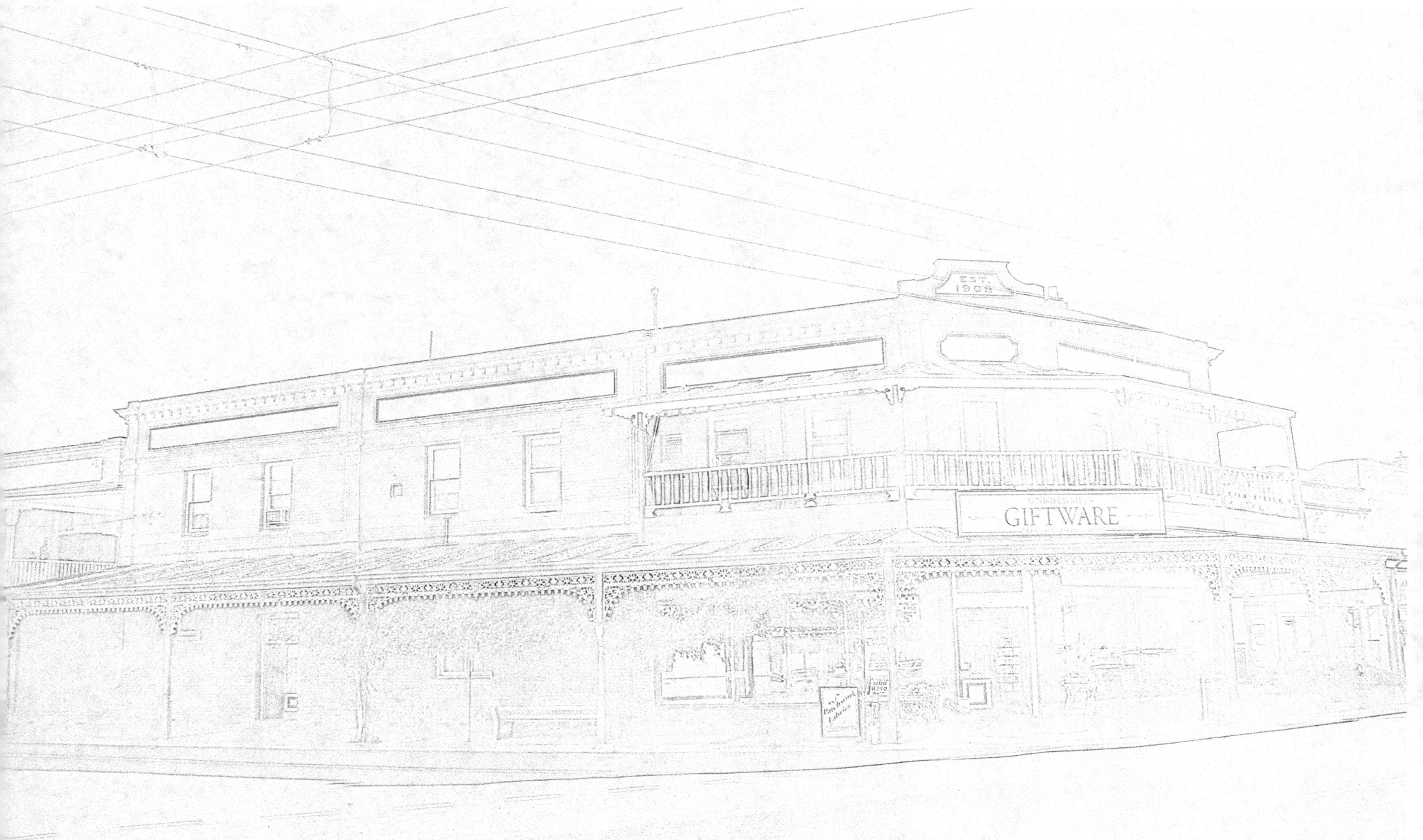
EST.
1902
GIFTWARE

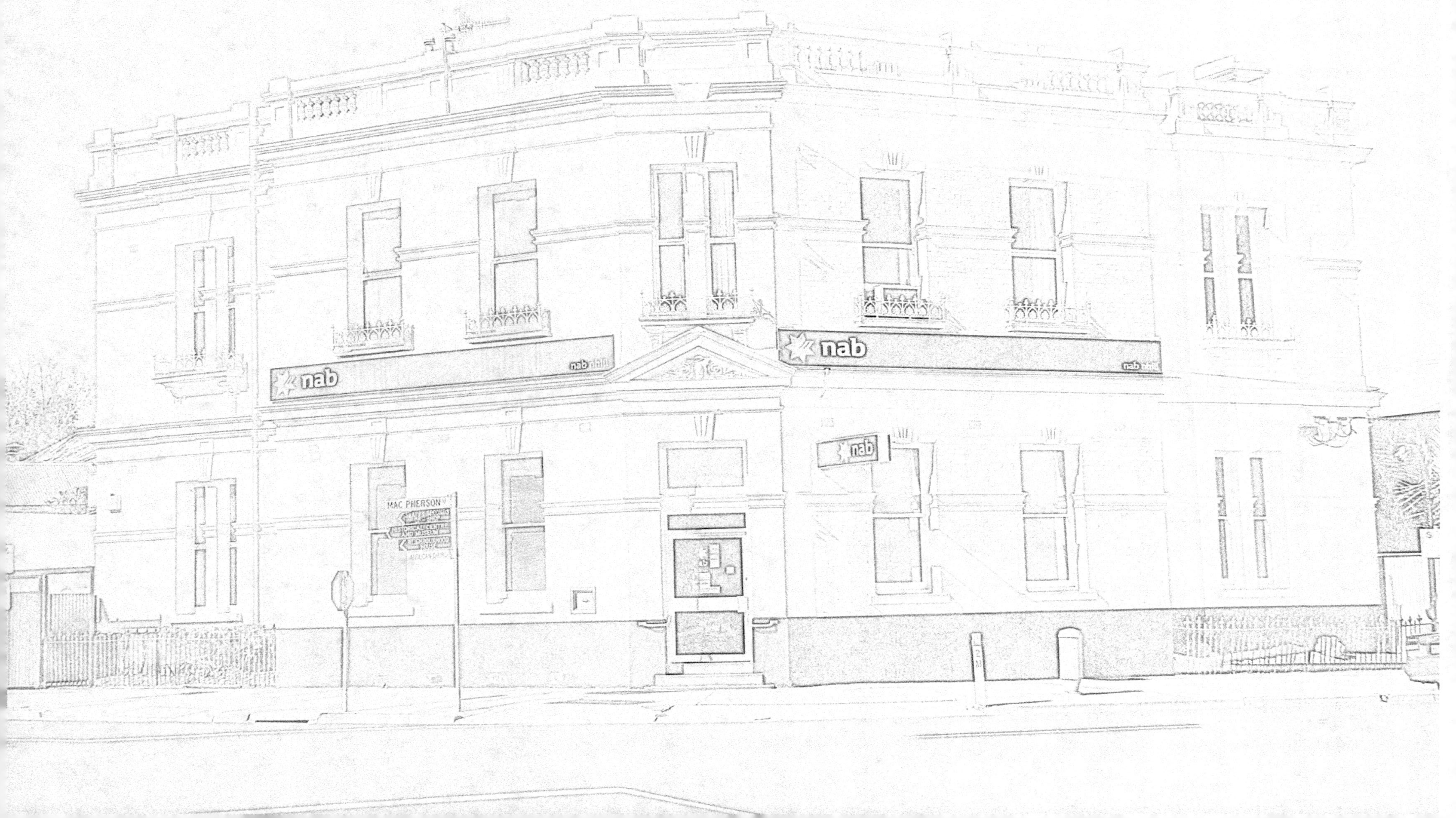
nab
nab
nab
MAC PHERSON

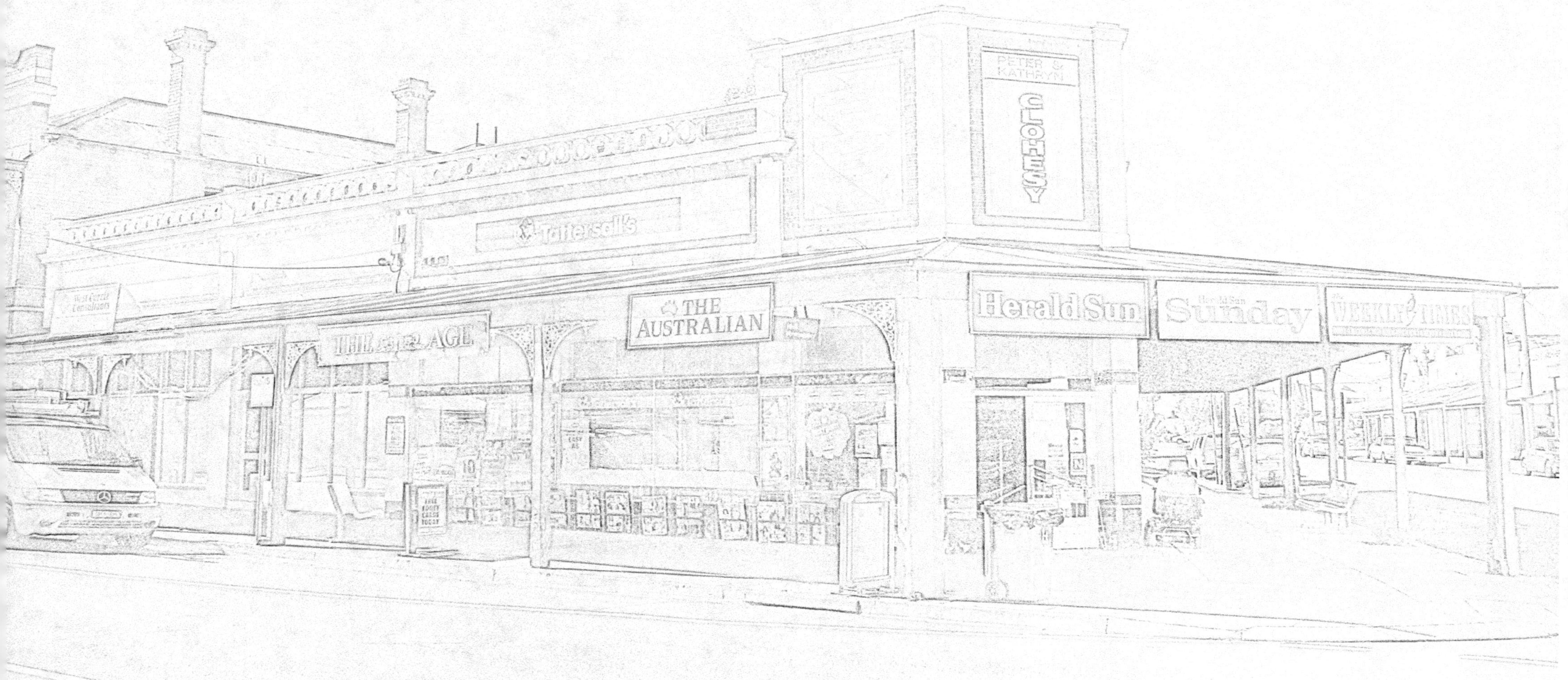
PETER & KATHRYN
CLOHESY
Tattersall's
THE AGE
THE AUSTRALIAN
Herald Sun
Sunday
WEEKLY TIMES

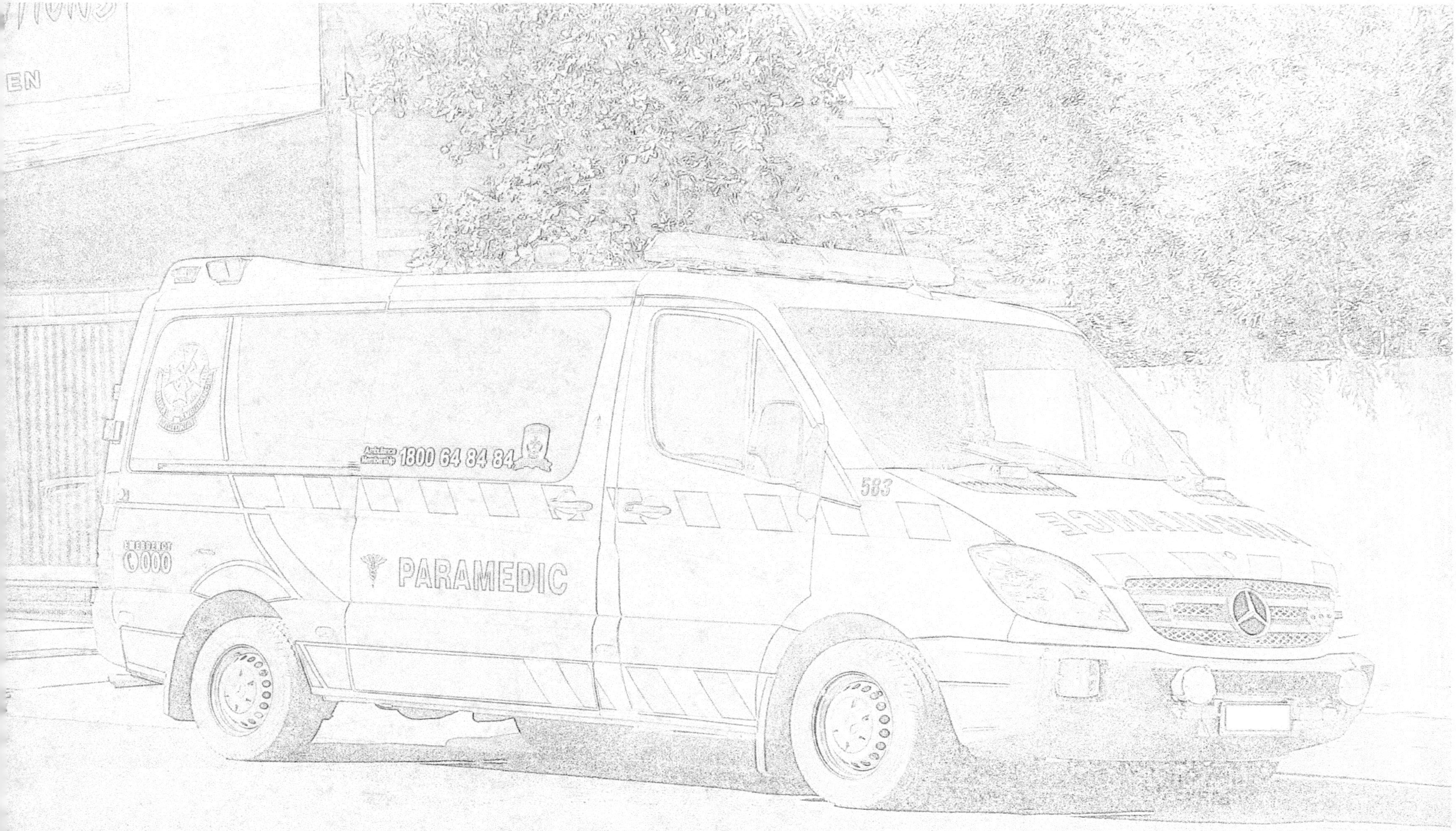
PARAMEDIC
1800 64 84 84
583
000

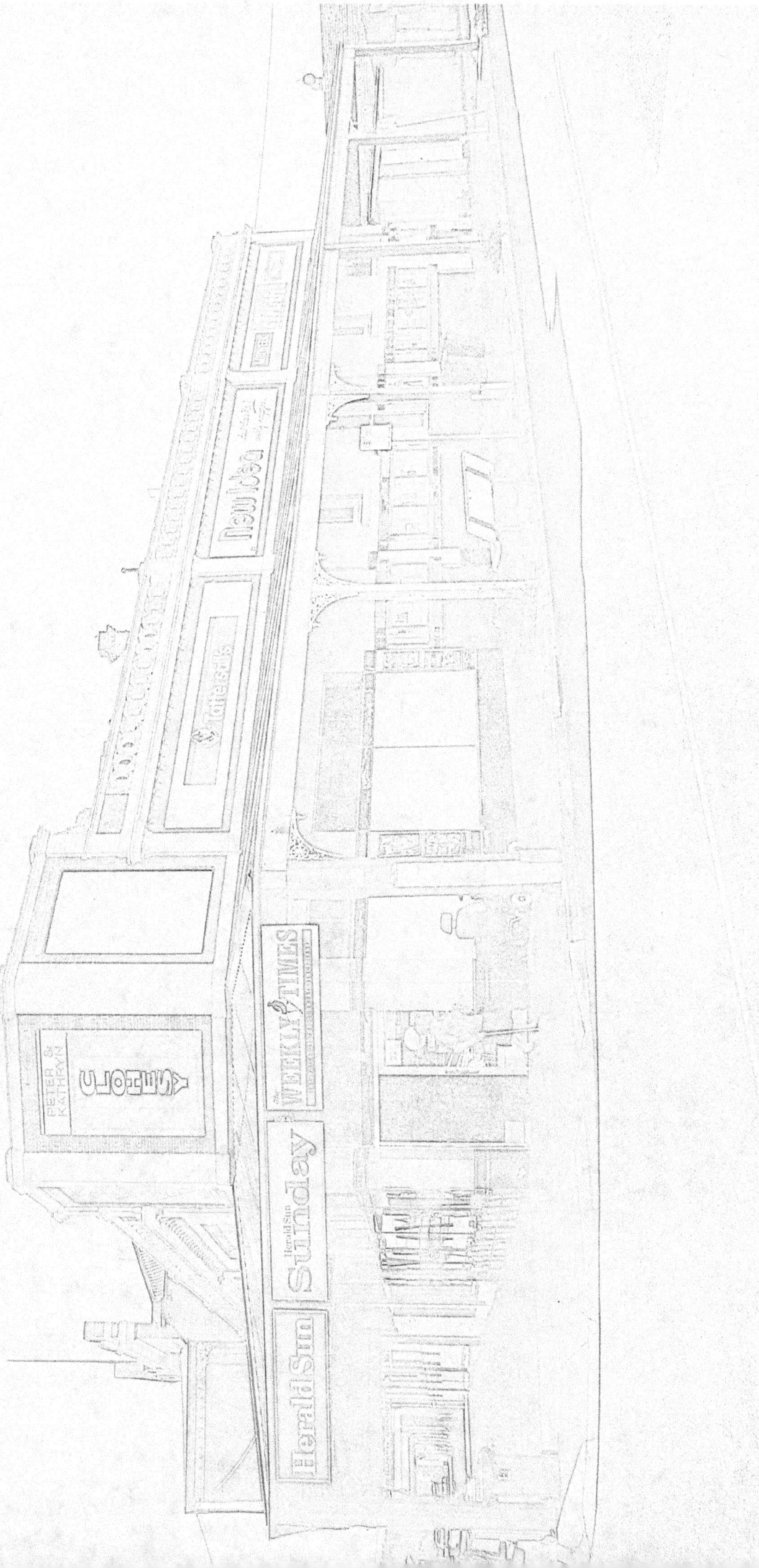
Herald Sun
Herald Sun Sunday
The WEEKLY TIMES
PETER & KATHRYN

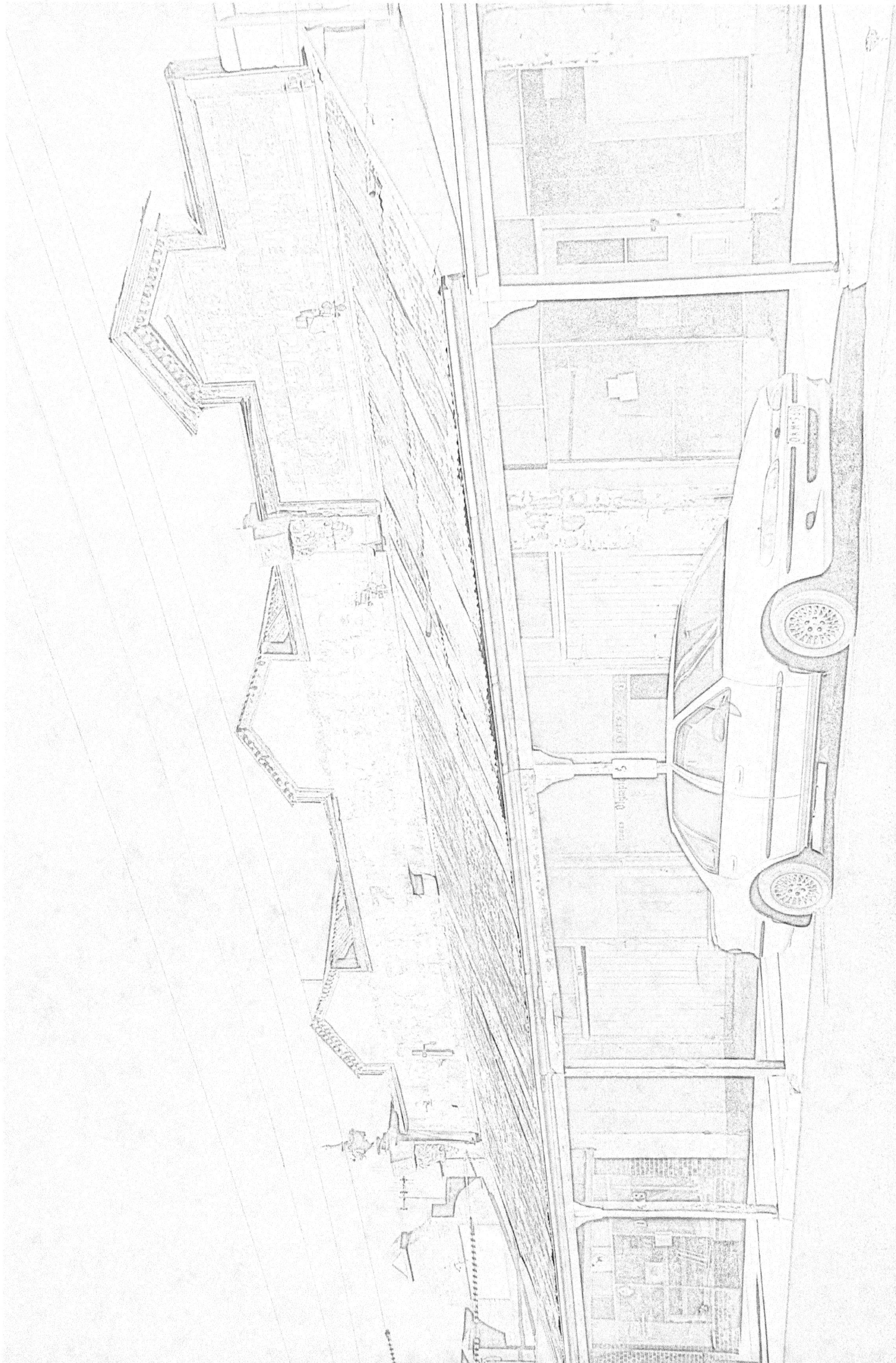

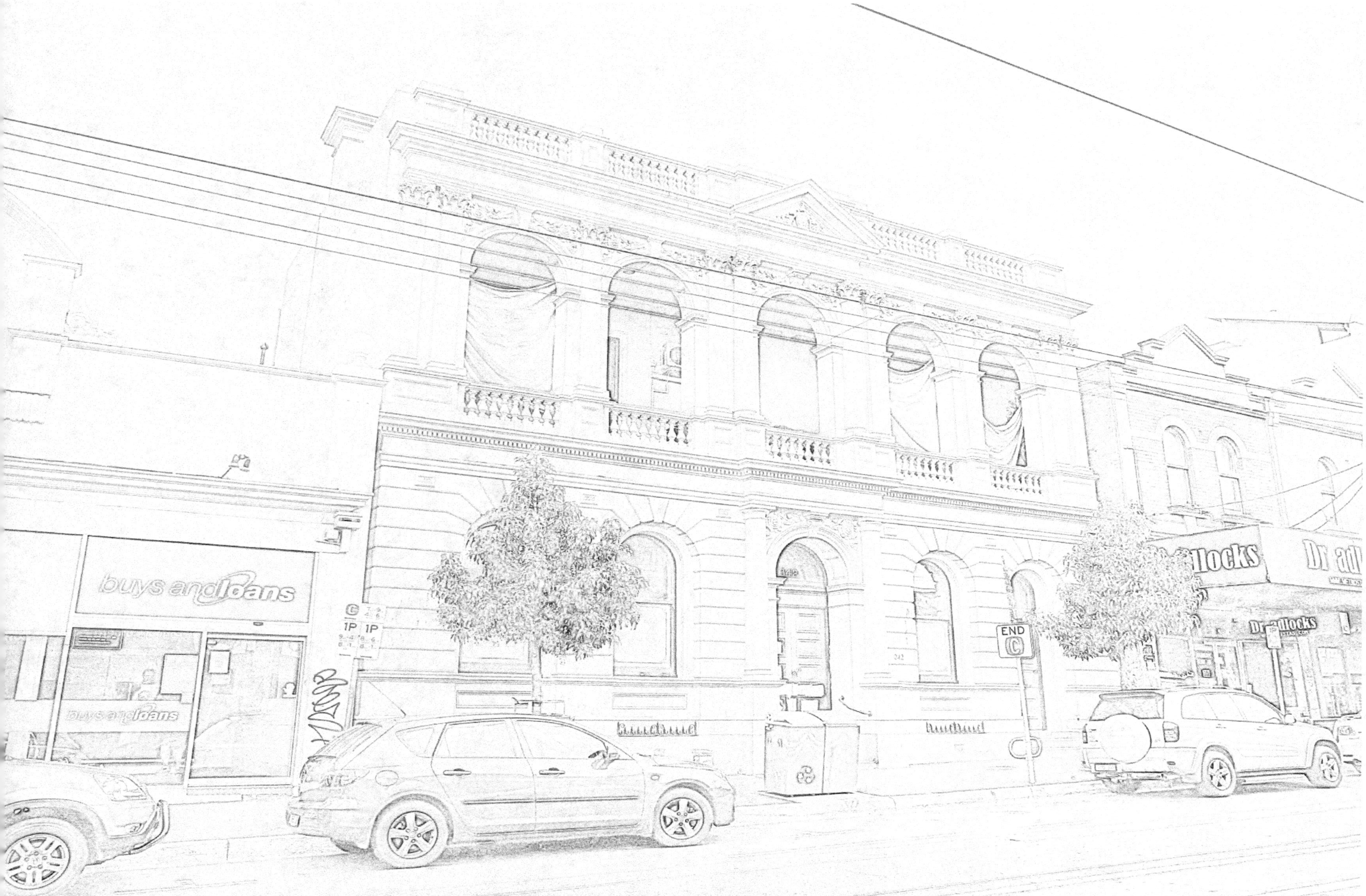
buys and loans
END
1P
1P
buys and loans

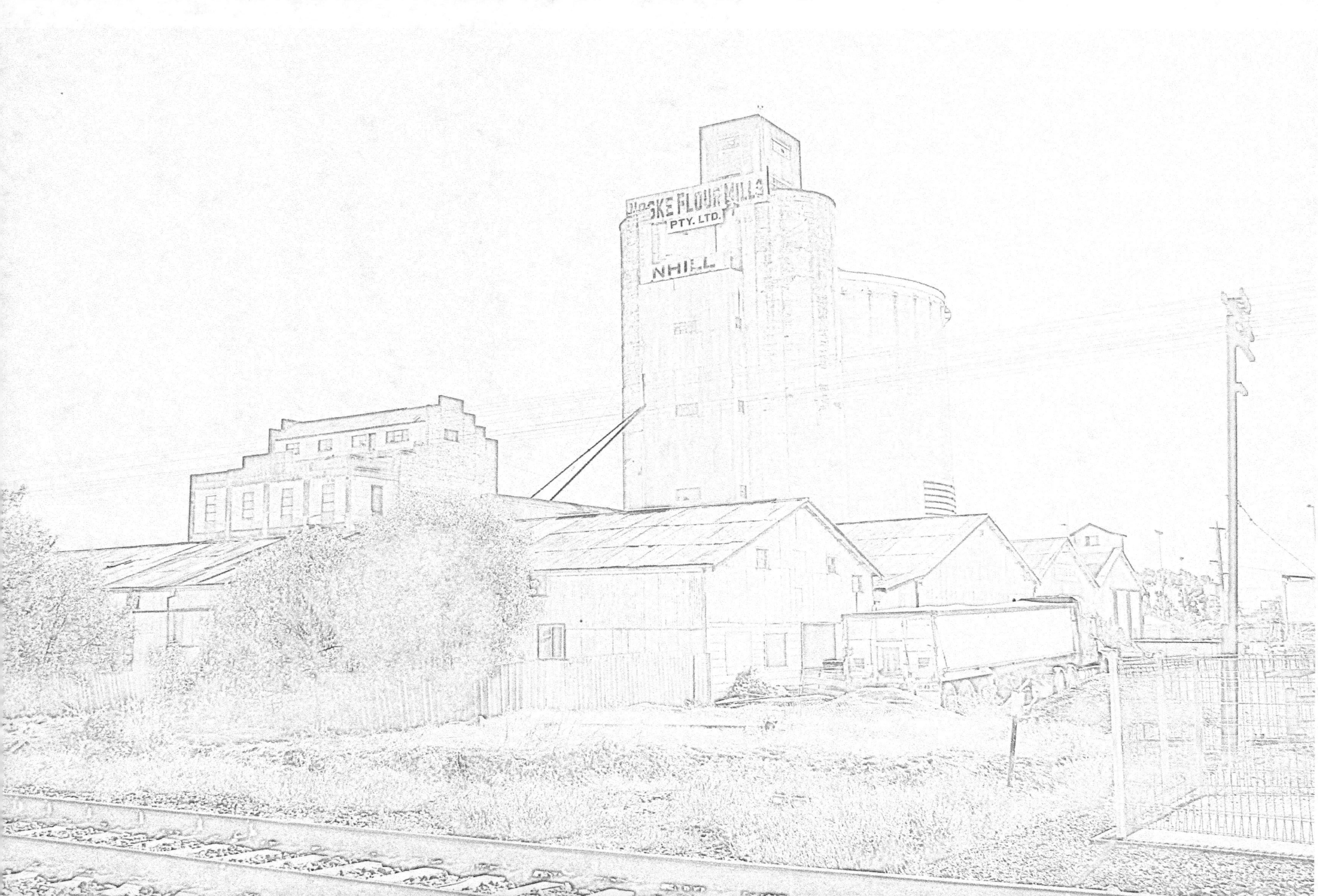
FLOUR MILLS
PTY. LTD.
NHILL

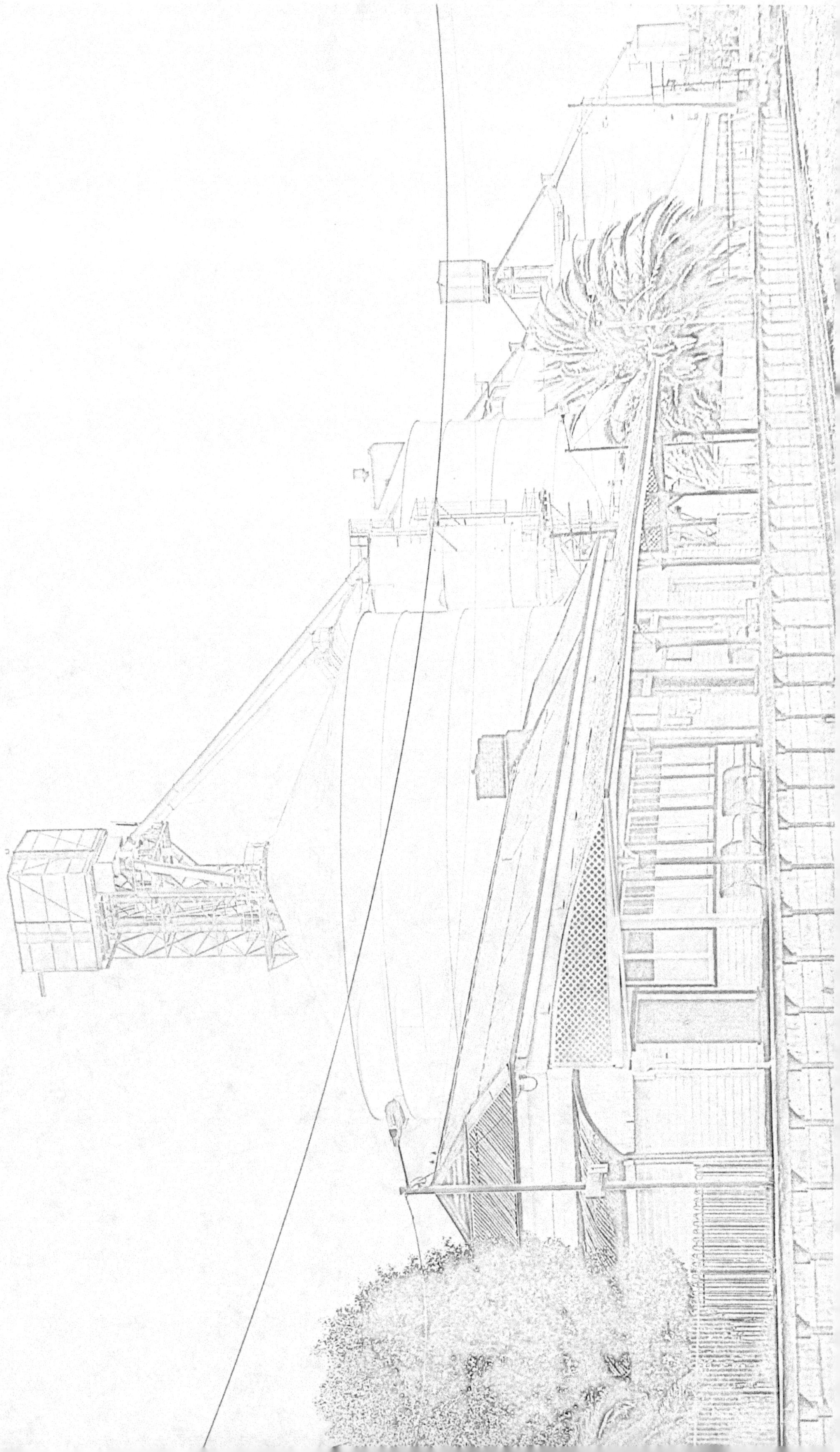

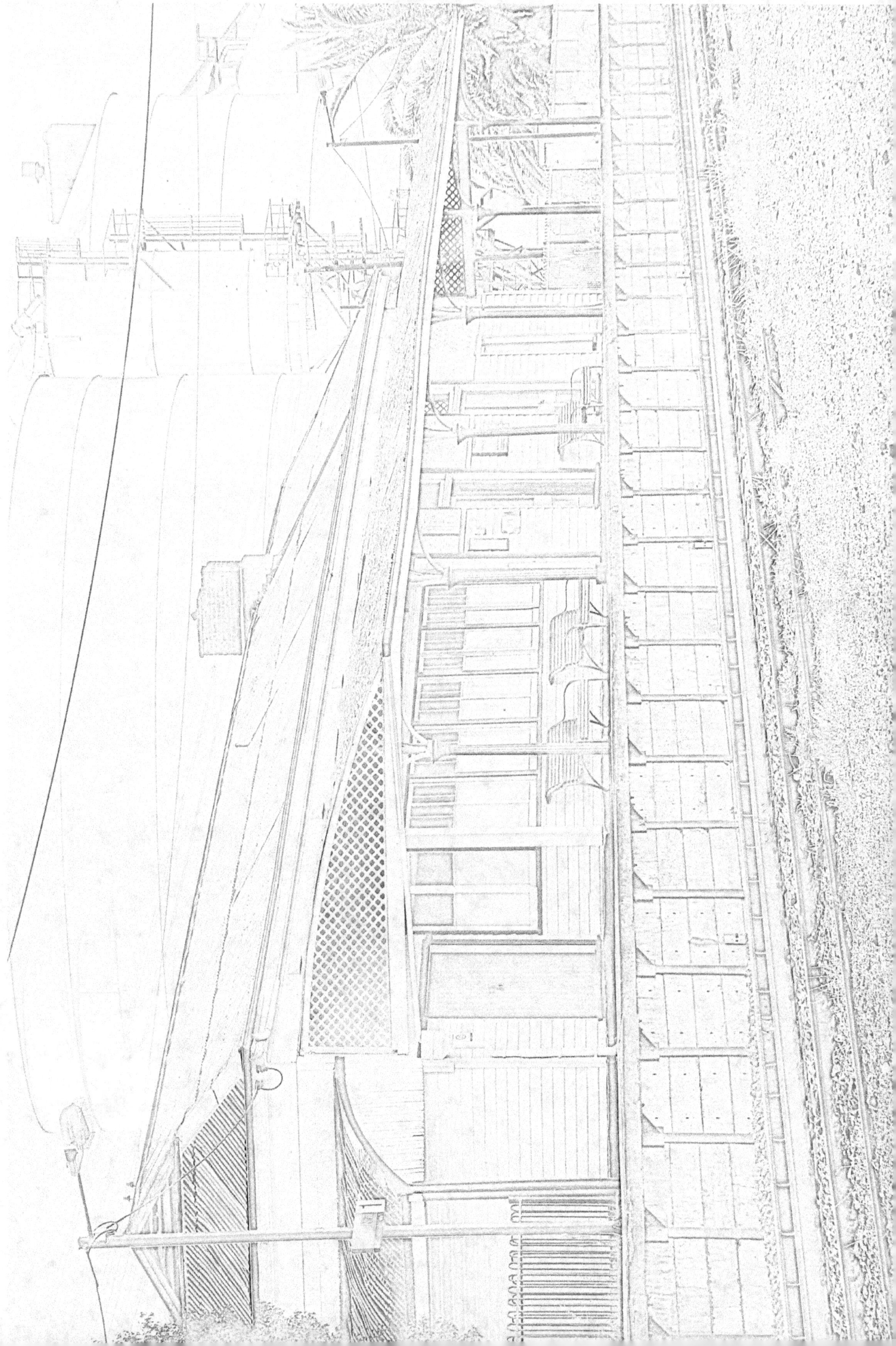

HOTEL/MOTEL ACCOMMODATION
Bottle
FAMILY BISTRO
Bar Grill
50

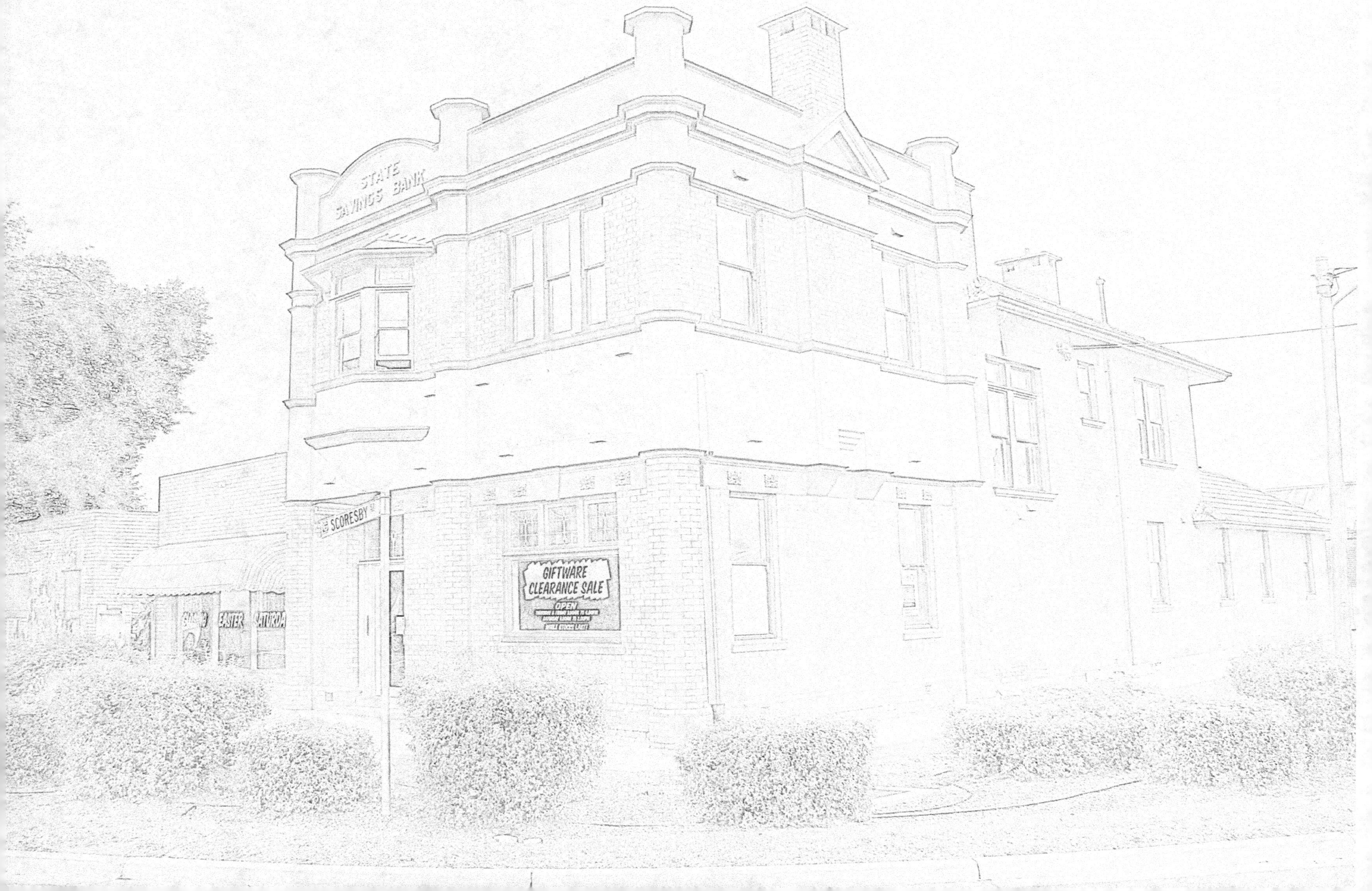
STATE
SAVINGS BANK
SCORESBY
GIFTWARE
CLEARANCE SALE
OPEN
EASTER

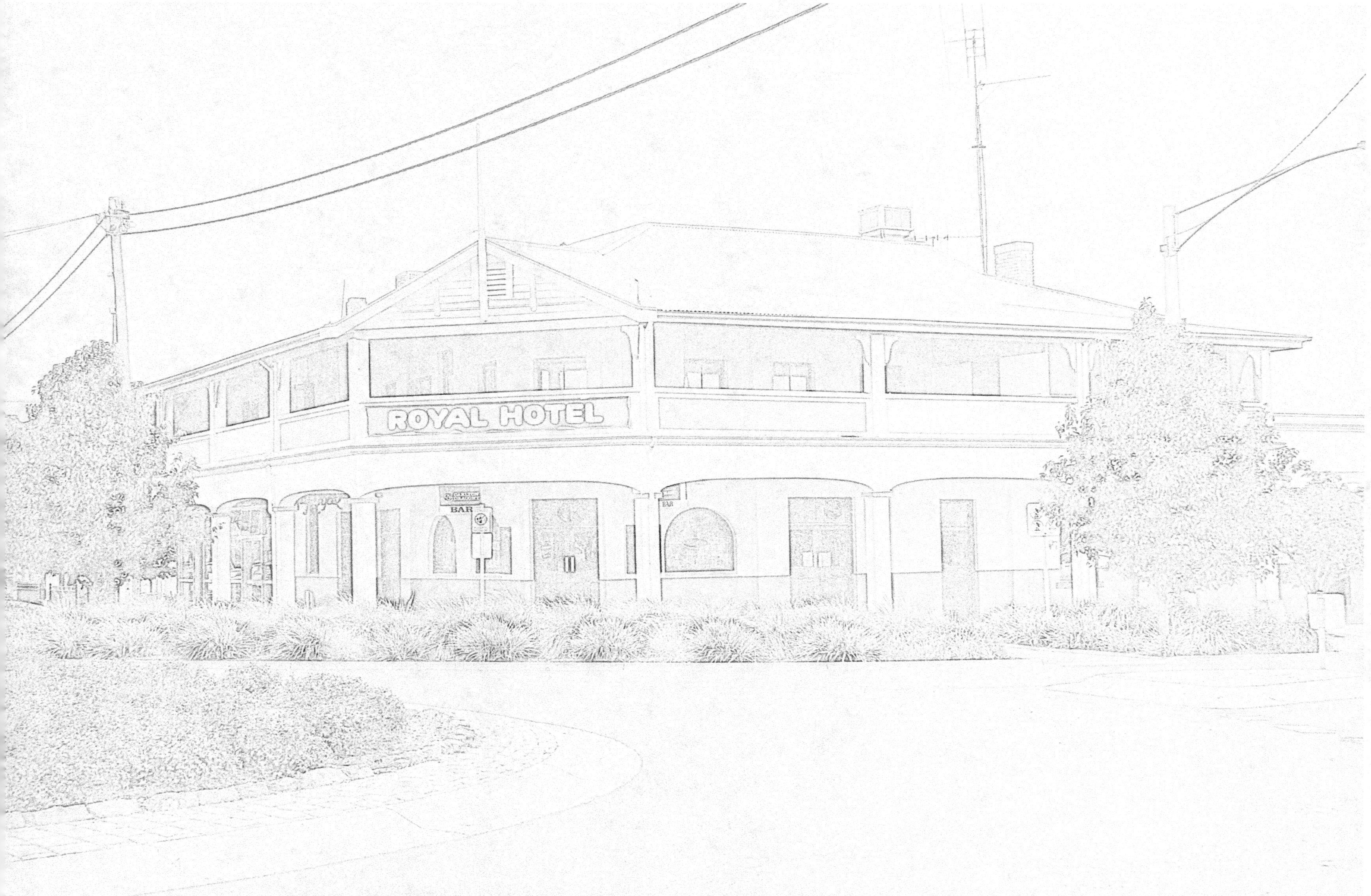
ROYAL HOTEL
BAR

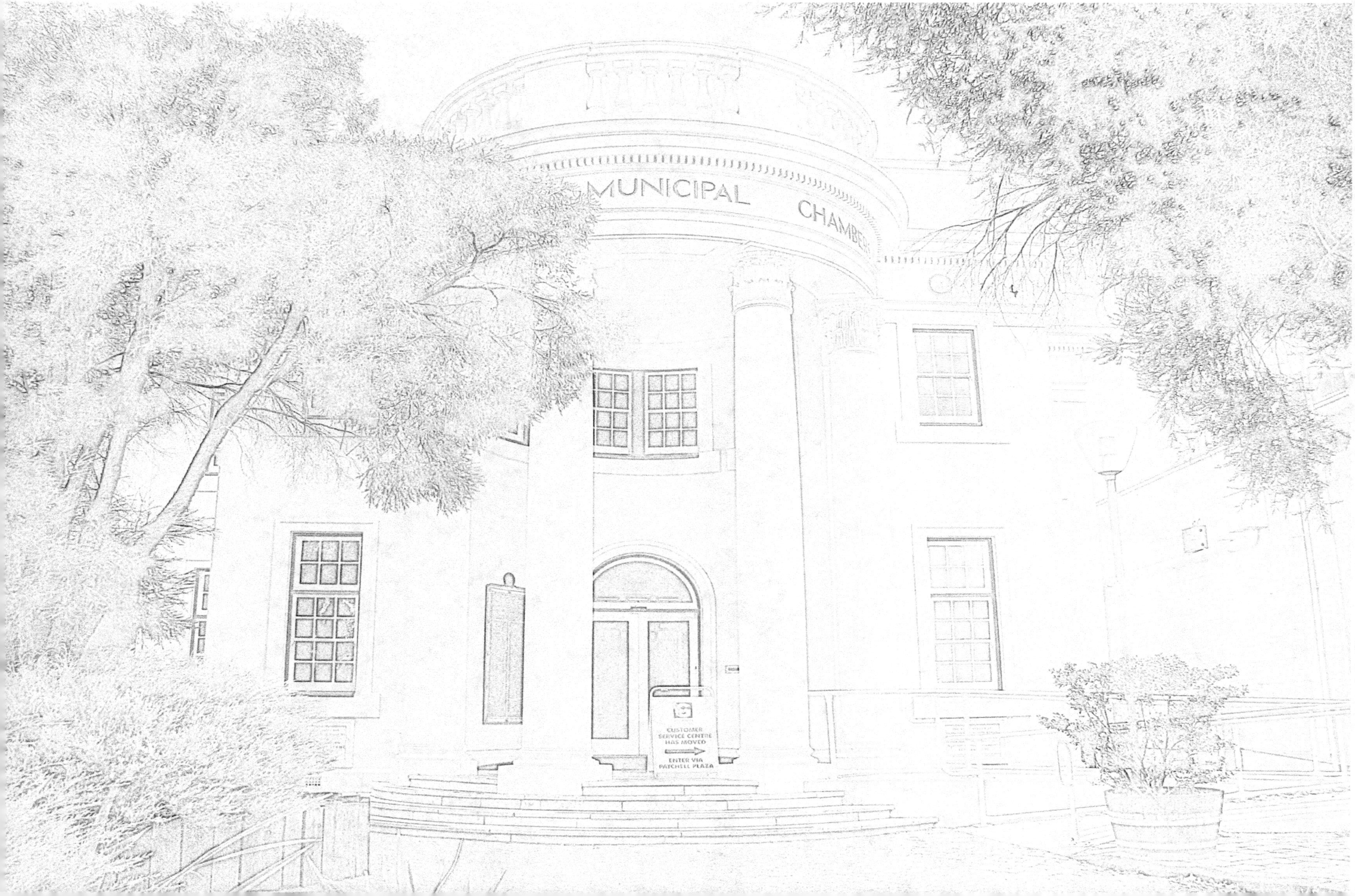
MUNICIPAL
CUSTOMER SERVICE CENTRE HAS MOVED
ENTER VIA PATCHELL PLAZA

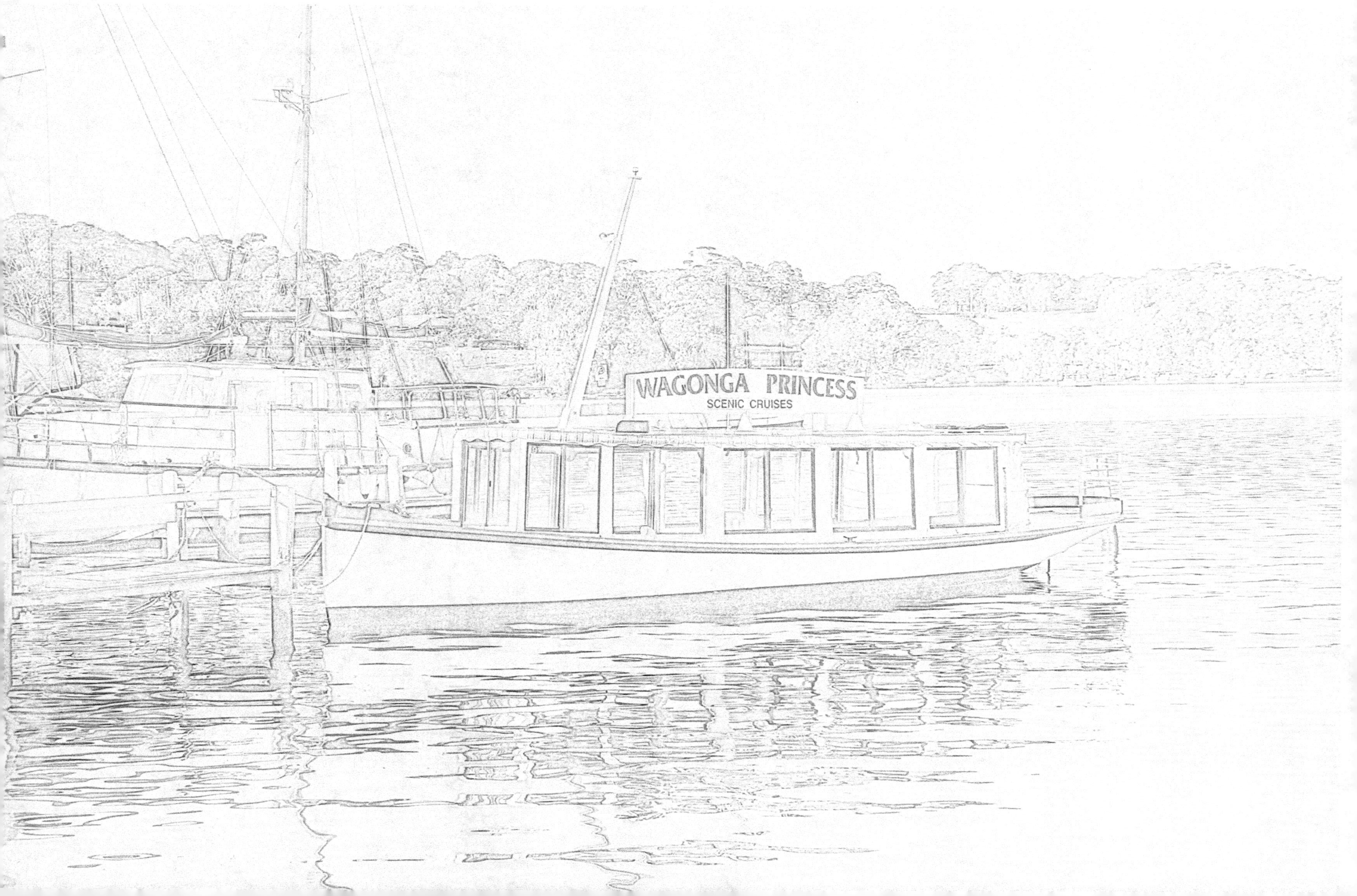
WAGONGA PRINCESS
SCENIC CRUISES

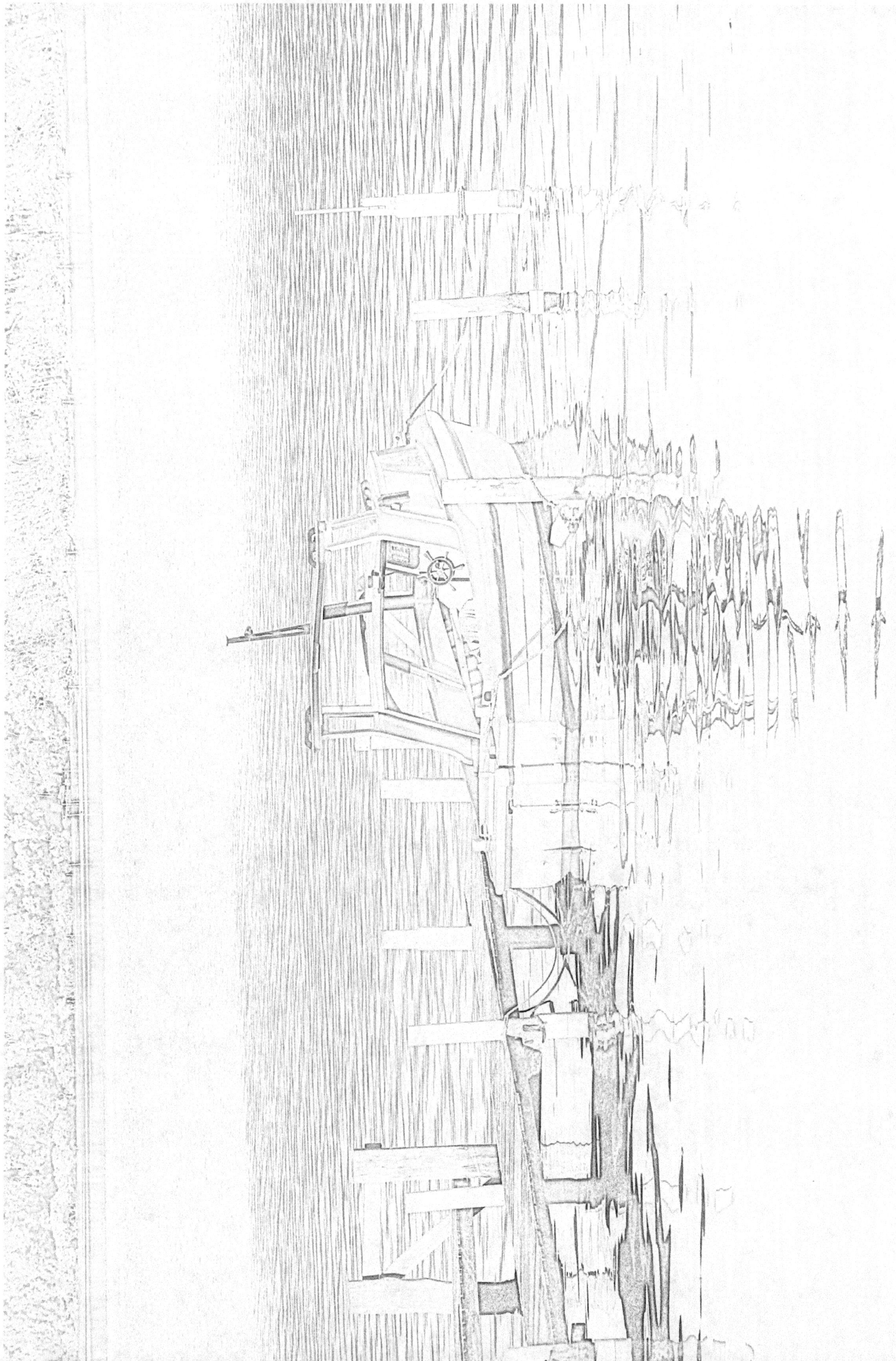

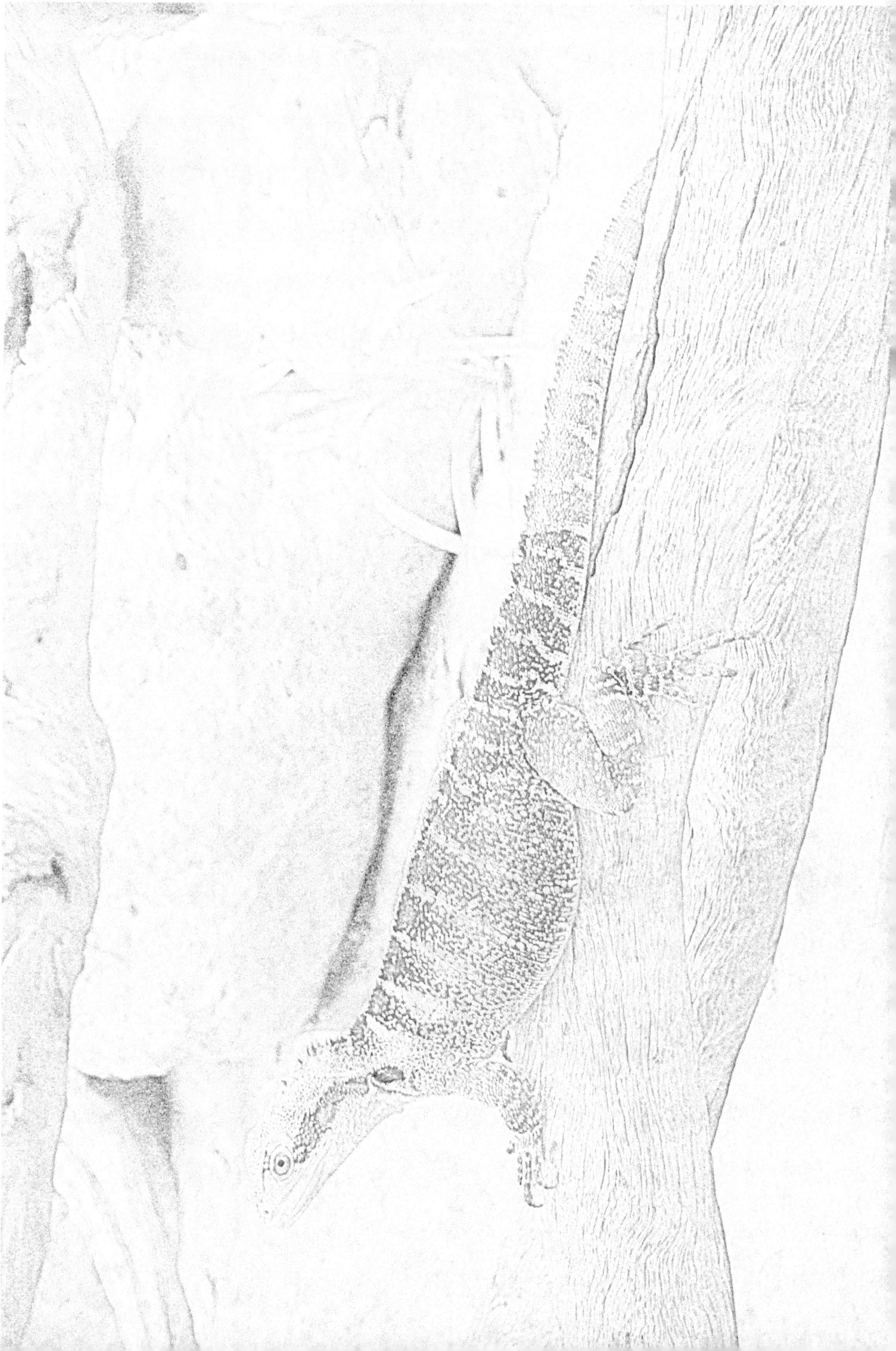

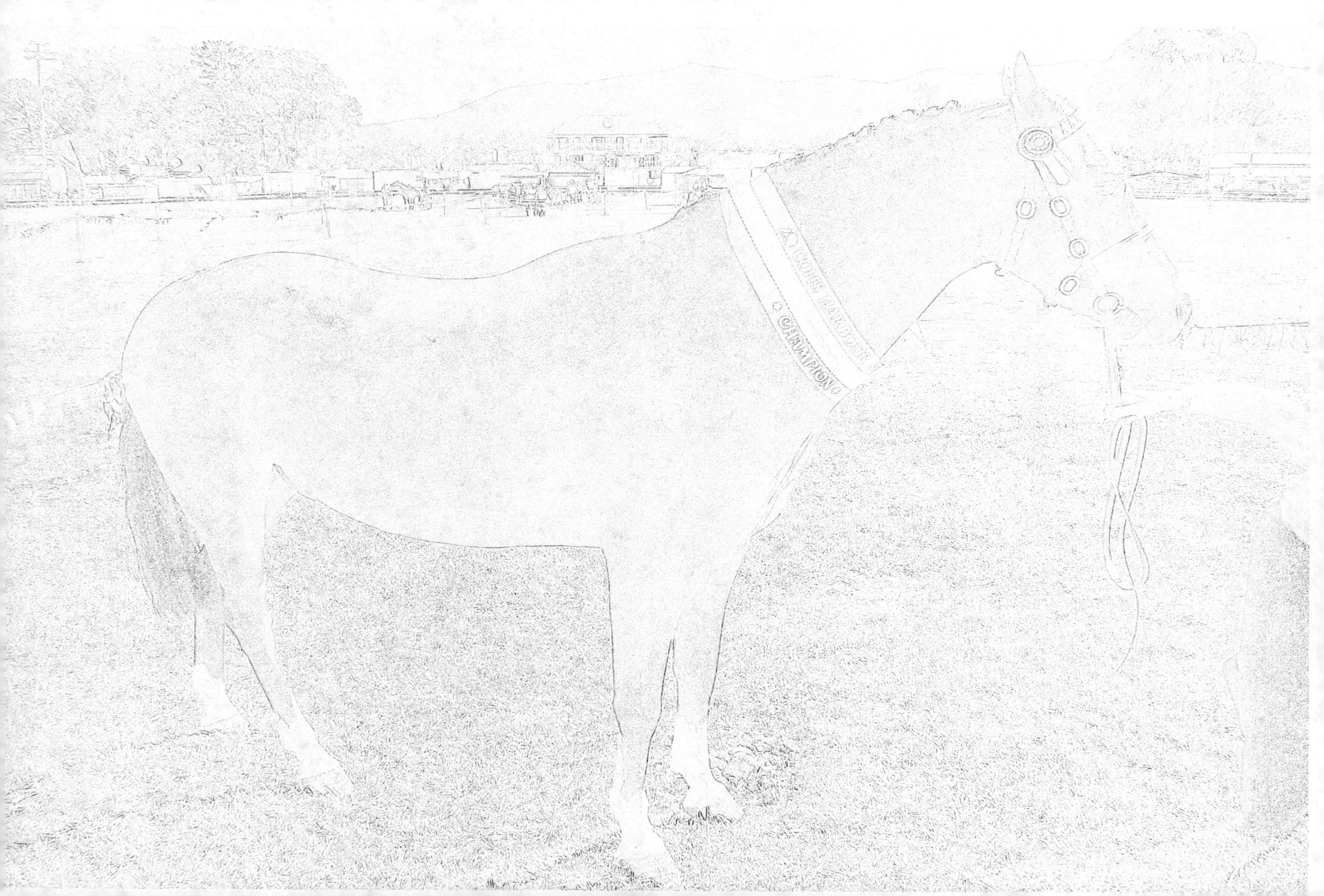
COFFS HARBOUR
CHAMPION

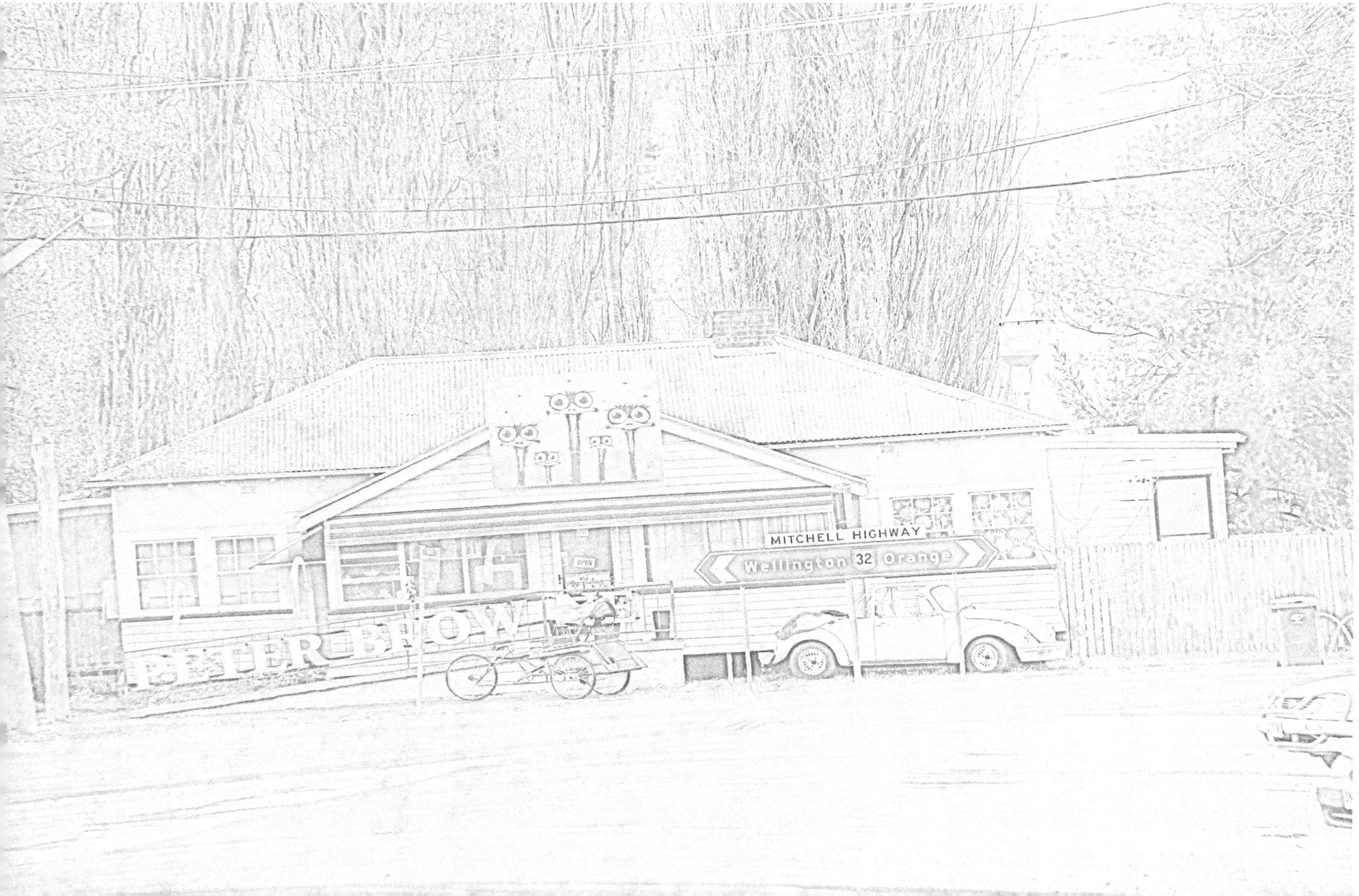
MITCHELL HIGHWAY
Wellington 32 Orange
OPEN
PETER BROW

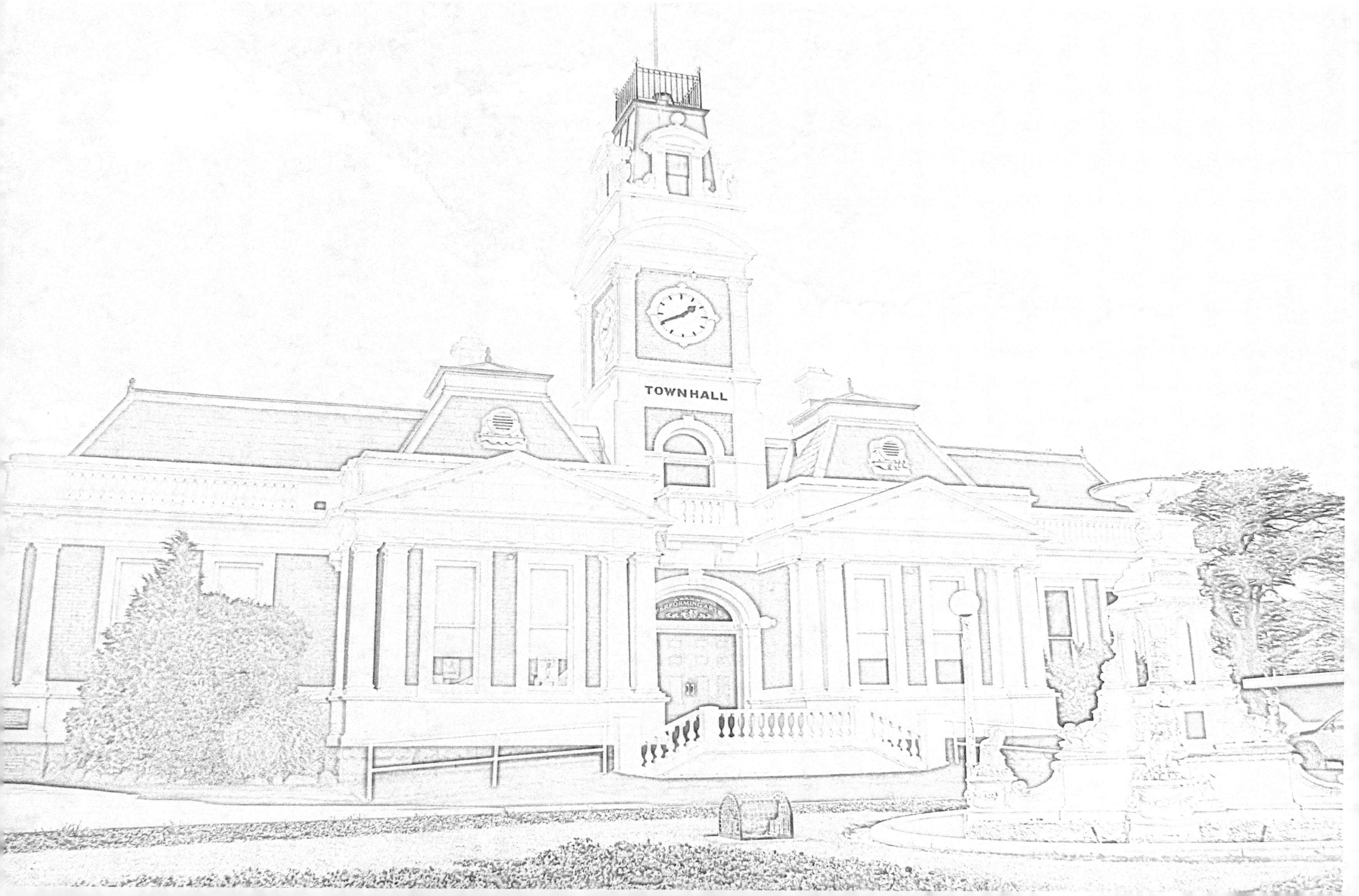
TOWN HALL

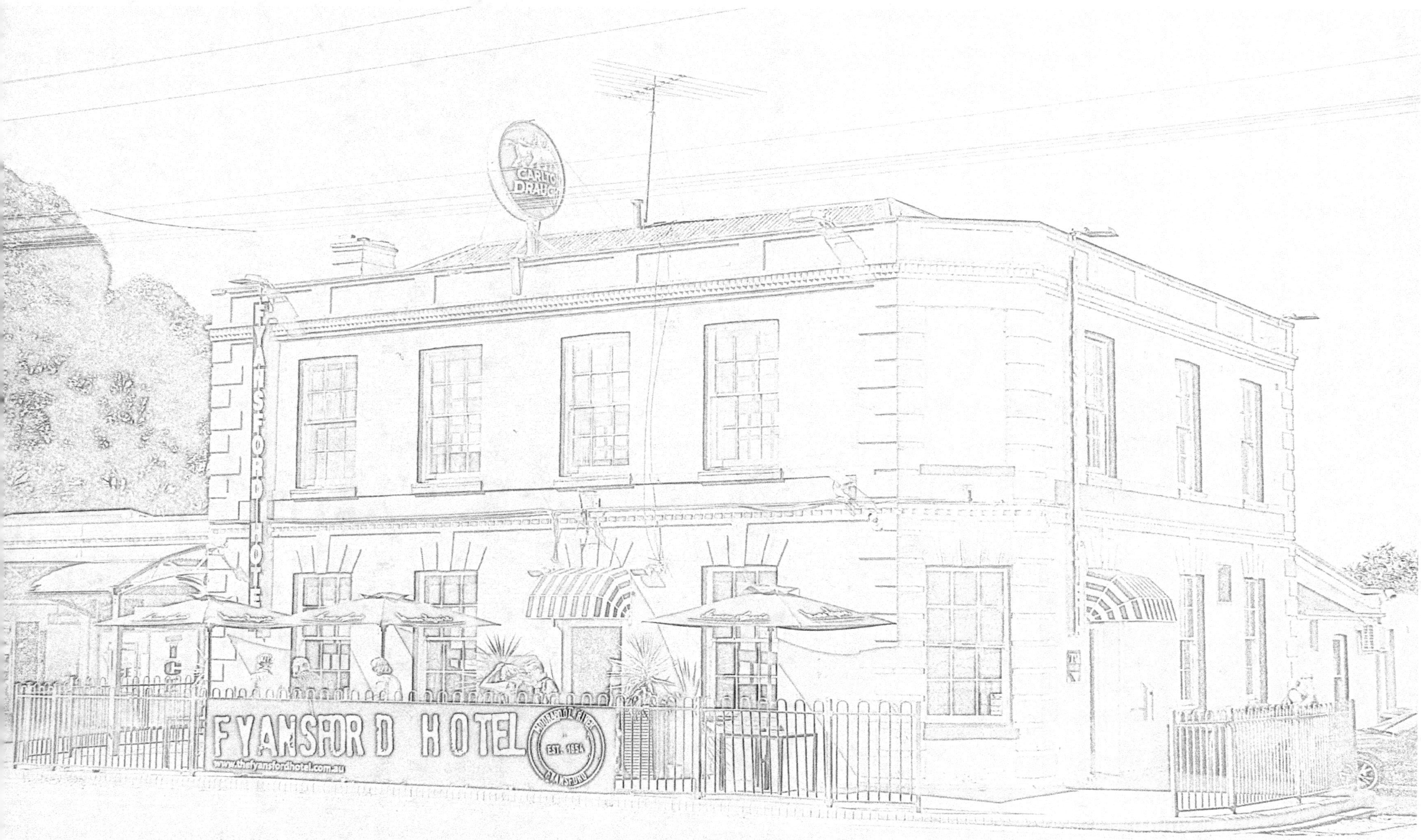

FYANSFORD HOTEL
www.thefyansfordhotel.com.au
EST. 1854

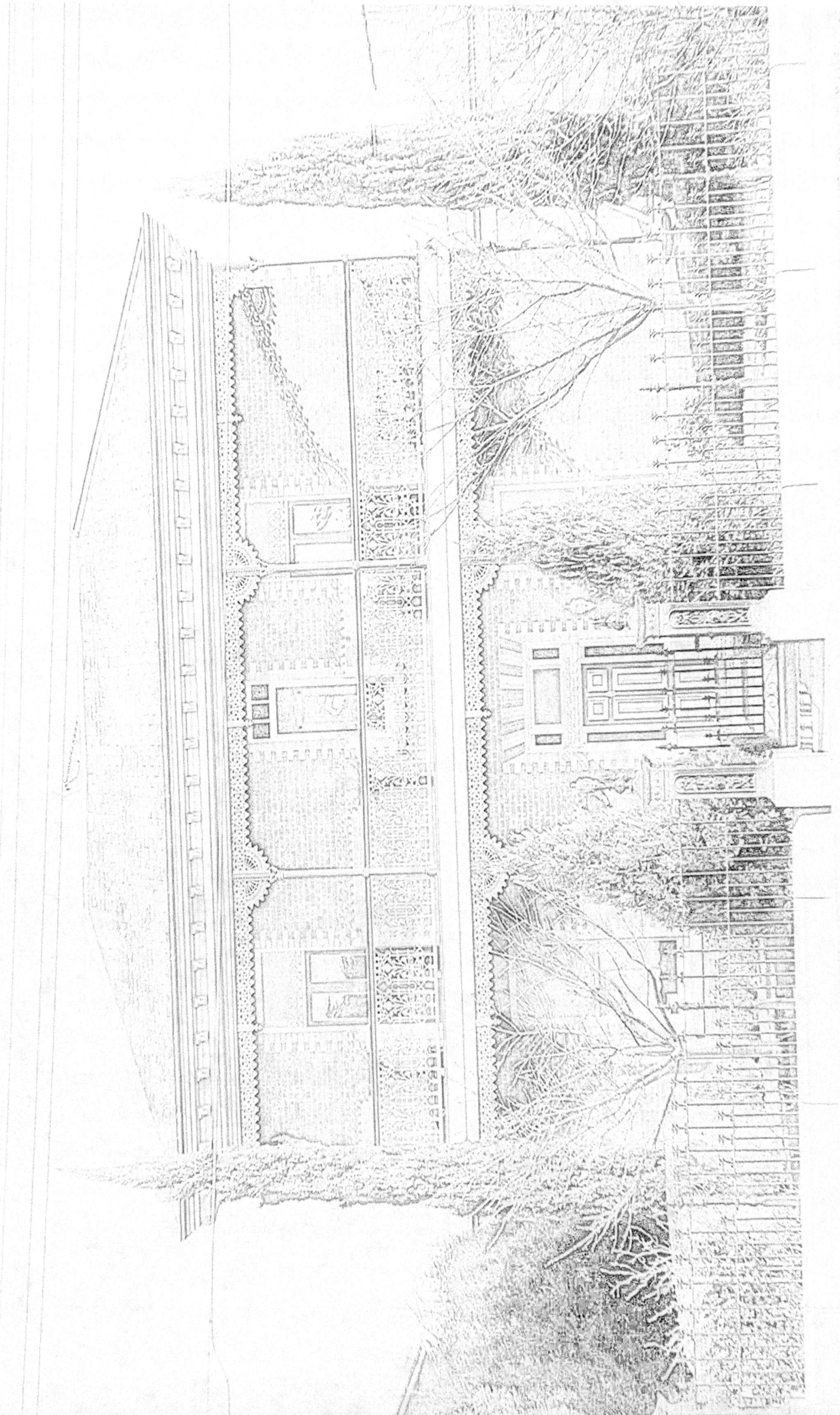

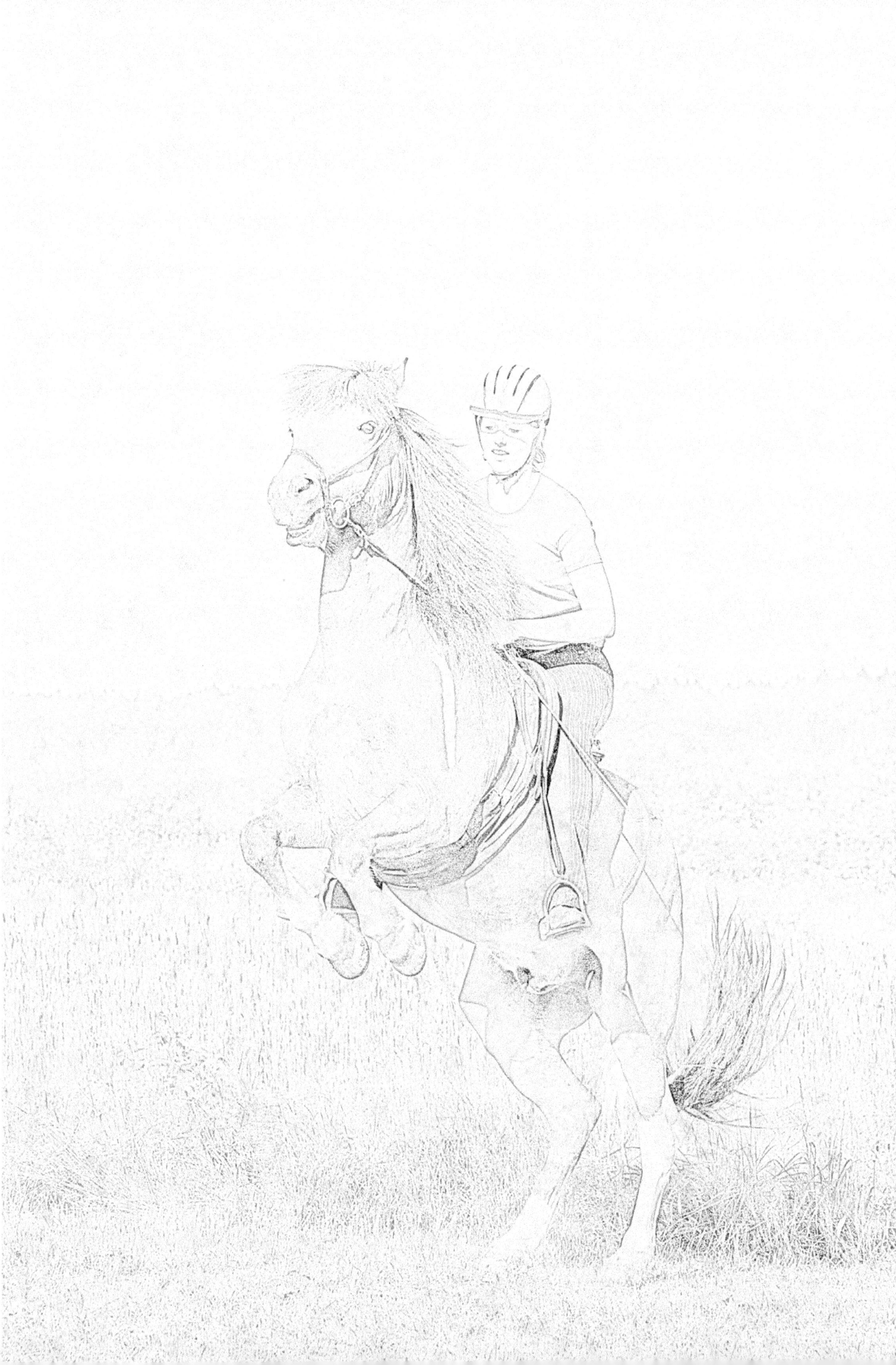

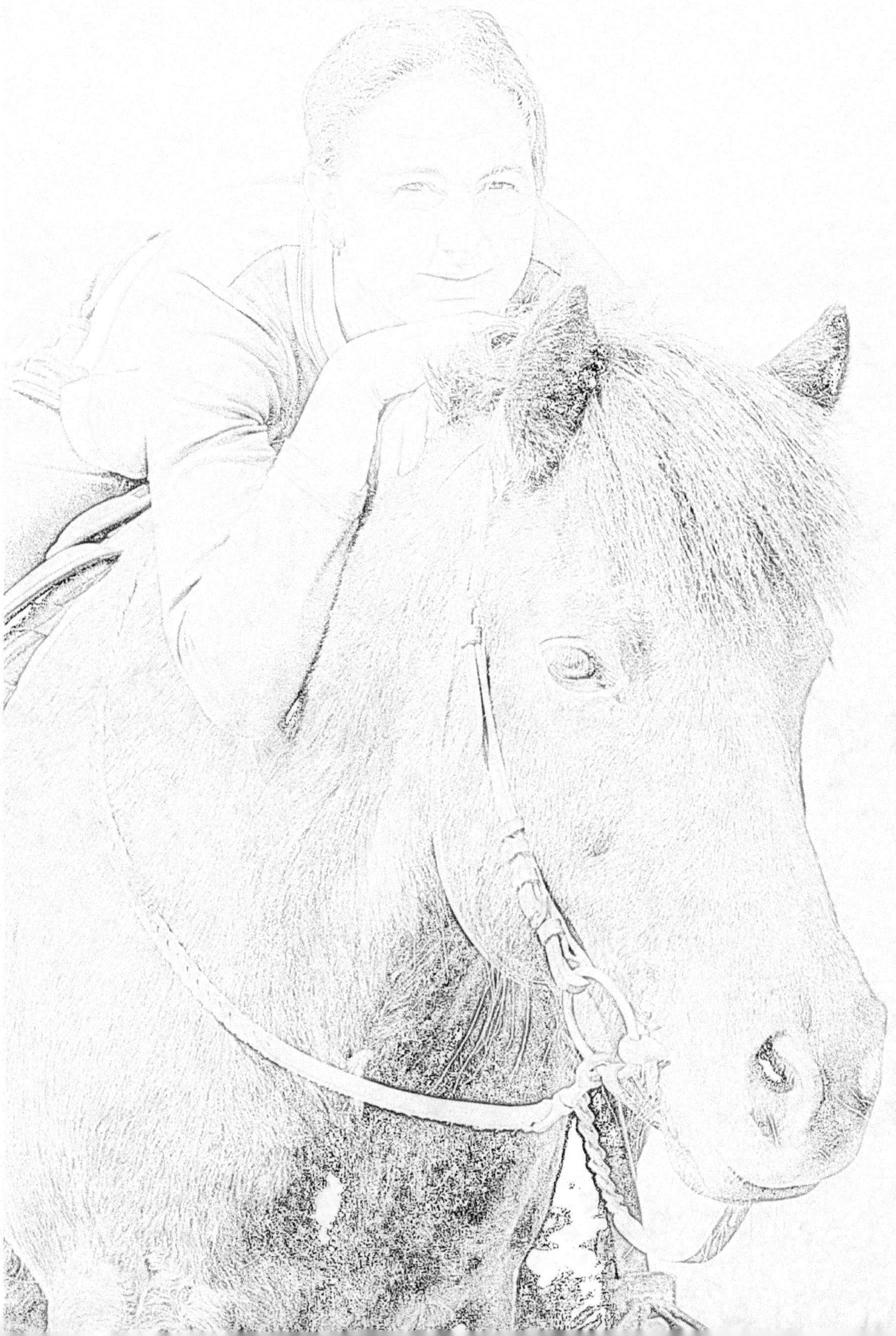

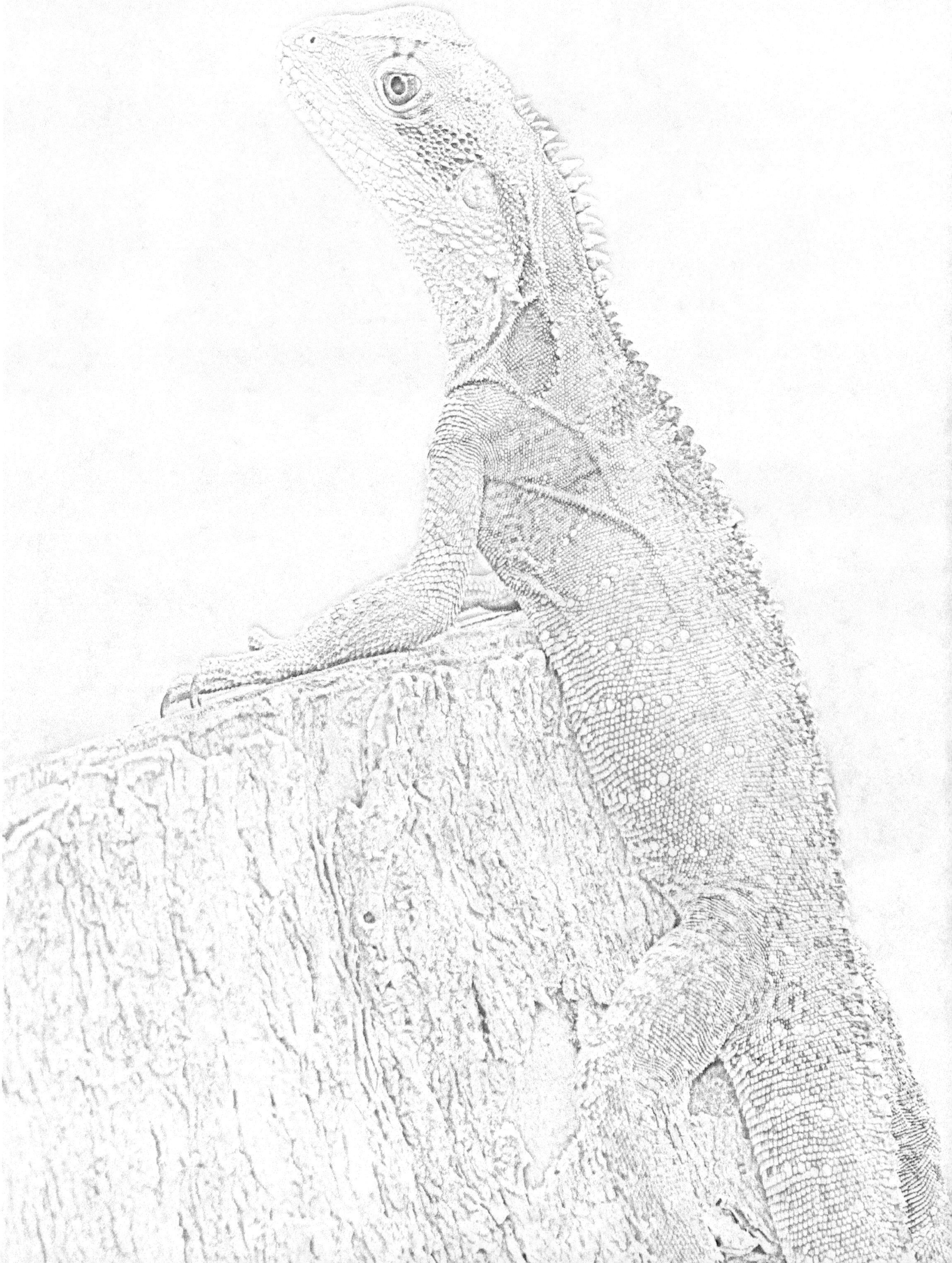

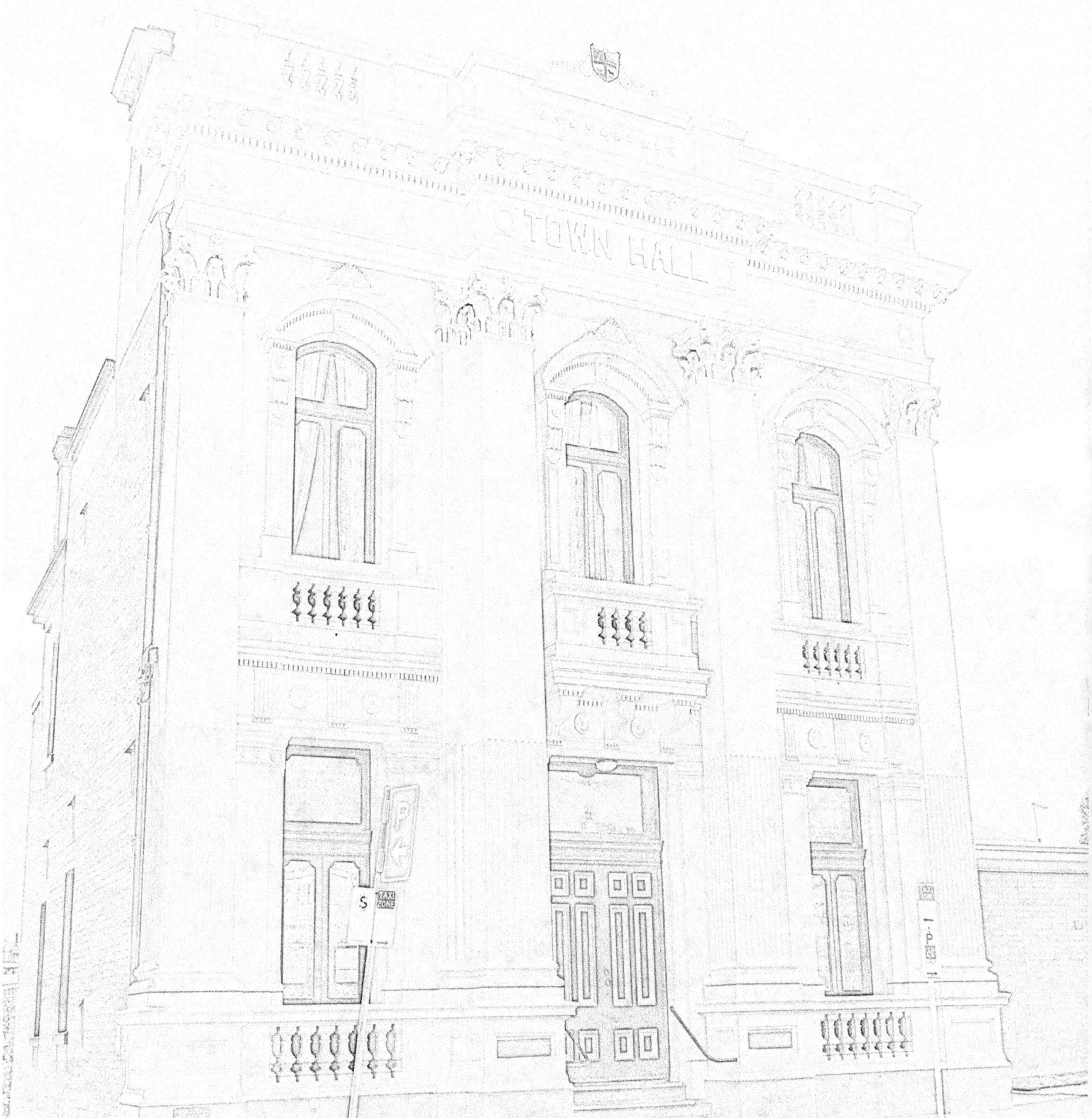
TOWN HALL
P
S
TAXI ZONE

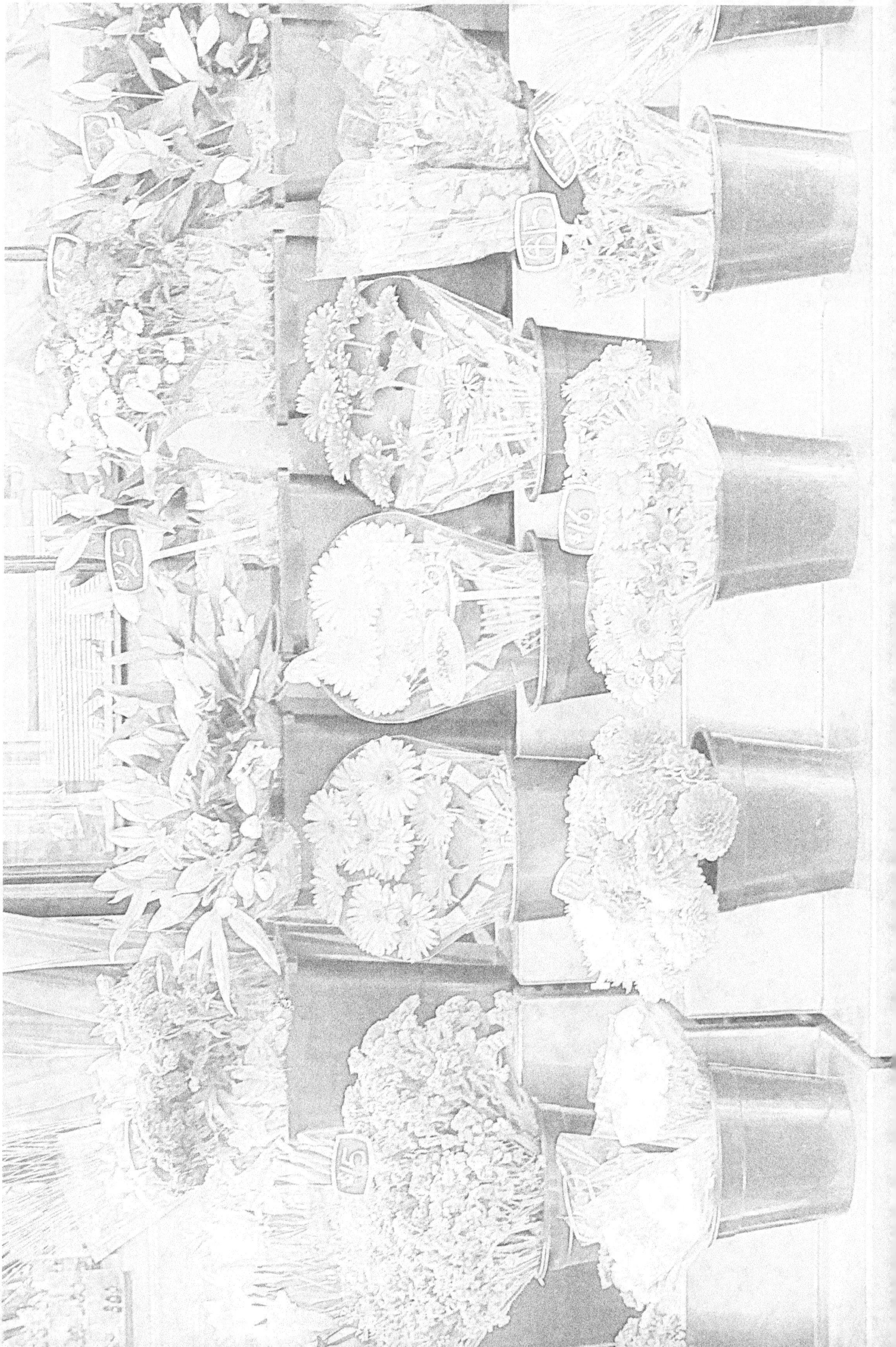

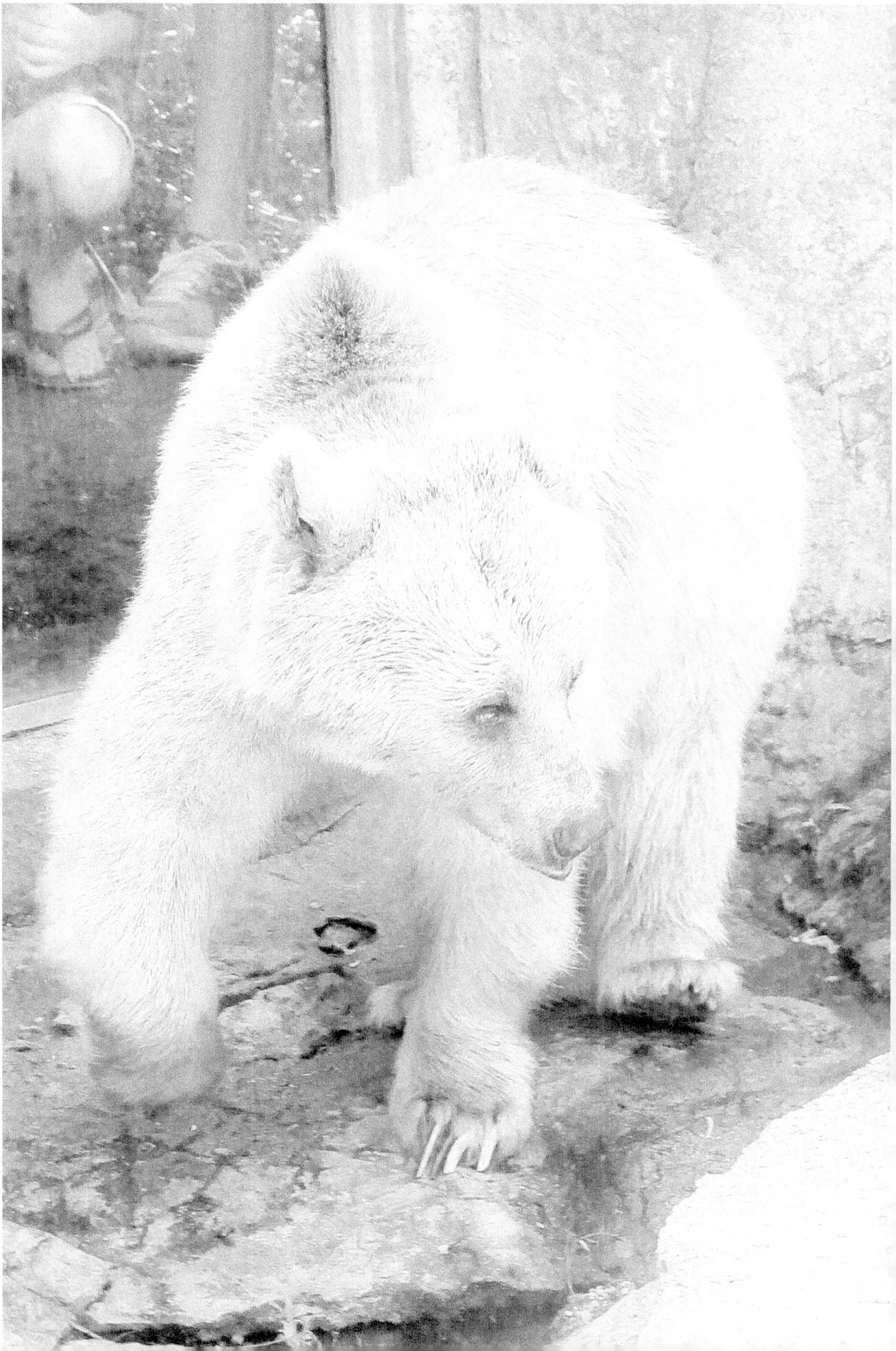

www.ingramcontent.com/pod-product-compliance
Lightning Source LLC
Chambersburg PA
CBHW081050180526
45170CB00005B/1750
* 9 7 8 0 3 5 9 8 2 2 9 2 8 *